From Your Friends At **The MAILBOX®**

OCTOBER

A MONTH OF IDEAS AT YOUR FINGERTIPS!

GRADES 4–6

WRITTEN BY
Becky Andrews, Chris Christensen, Irving P. Crump, Ann Fisher, Beth Gress, Peggy W. Hambright, Mary Lou Schlosser, Christine A. Thuman, Patricia Twohey

EDITED BY
Becky Andrews, Lynn Bemer Coble, Jennifer Rudisill, Gina Sutphin

ILLUSTRATED BY
Marilynn G. Barr, Jennifer T. Bennett, Pam Crane, Teresa Davidson, Susan Hodnett, Sheila Krill, Barry Slate, Donna K. Teal

COVER DESIGNED BY
Jennifer T. Bennett

©1996 by THE EDUCATION CENTER, INC.
All rights reserved except as here noted.
ISBN# 1-56234-128-6

Manufactured in the United States
10 9 8 7 6 5 4 3 2 1

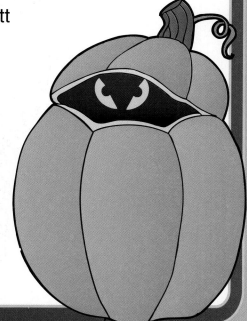

TABLE OF CONTENTS

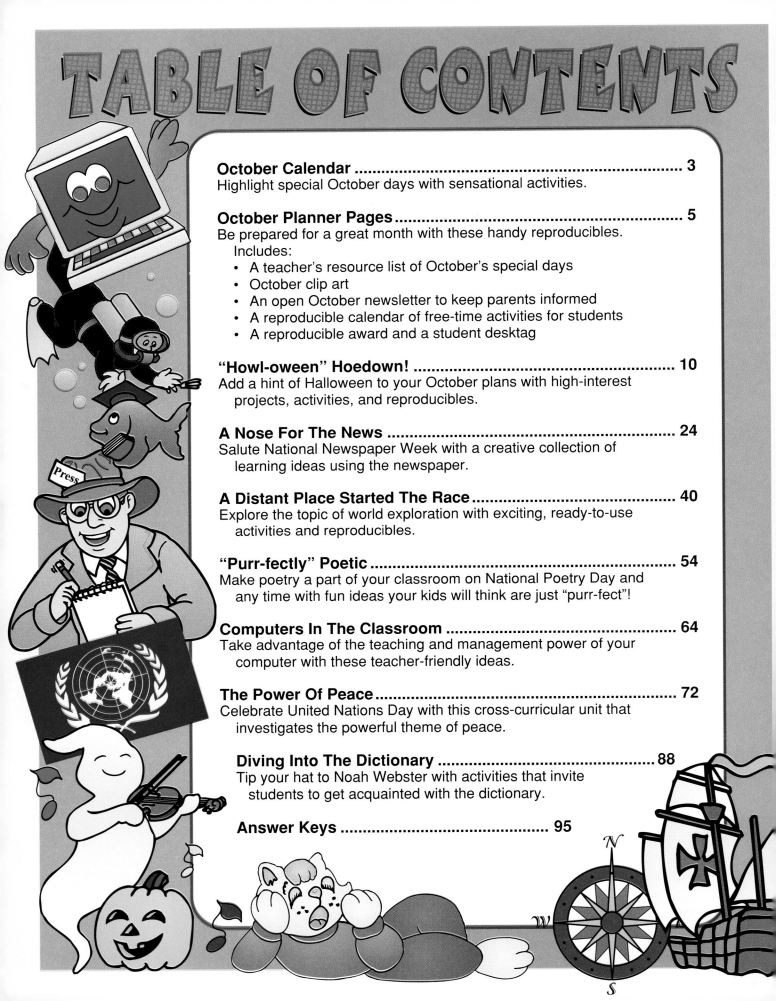

October Calendar

Consumer Information Month

Get ready to raise your students' consumer I.Q.s during Consumer Information Month in October. The purpose of this special month-long observance is to promote reliable information sources that help consumers acquire quality products or services. During October, acquaint your students with *Zillions,* a magazine for kids published by Consumers Union (which also publishes *Consumer Reports).* Obtain copies of this magazine for each group of students to peruse. Have each group choose one article to evaluate and share with the class.

2—Happy Birthday, Charlie Brown!

Charles M. Schulz's beloved "Peanuts" comic-strip characters celebrate their birthday on this day. Charlie Brown—the boy who fails at everything—and the cartoon's other characters now appear in 2,400 newspapers in 68 countries. Cut out three or four short "Peanuts" comic strips from newspapers. Glue the strips to a piece of paper; then white-out the dialogue and duplicate a copy of the page for each student. Have students fill in the speech bubbles with their own dialogue.

4—Anniversary Of *Sputnik's* Launch

On this day in 1957, the first successful man-made earth satellite, *Sputnik I,* was launched into space by the USSR. This satellite transmitted radio signals to earth for 21 days and marked the beginning of the space age. Ask your students to speculate about how history would be different if this event had never happened.

National Pet Peeve Week

National Pet Peeve Week, observed October 9–13, gives everyone a chance to make others aware of life's little annoyances—in the hope of changing some of them. Discuss with students the things that get on their nerves (but caution them not to use anyone's name when describing a pet peeve). Then have each student list five pet peeves and include a positive suggestion for coping with each annoyance.

10—Pledge Of Allegiance Written

Francis Bellamy wrote the Pledge Of Allegiance for the October 10, 1892, issue of *The Youth's Companion* magazine. The pledge was written for the purpose of instilling a sense of patriotism and loyalty in immigrants' children. School systems throughout America soon adopted it. Explain the pledge, phrase by phrase, to your class. Then ask each student to use it as a model for writing a class pledge.

(Turn the page for more…)

14—Birthday Of The Peace Corps

The idea for the Peace Corps—an independent overseas volunteer program of the U.S. government—was proposed to the public by presidential candidate John F. Kennedy on this date in 1960. Its volunteers serve two-year stints helping people in poor countries to help themselves. Discuss with students the characteristics a Peace Corps volunteer would have to possess. On an index card, have each student list ways that he could help a country in need as a Peace Corps volunteer.

24—Birthday Of Anton van Leeuwenhoek

Anton van Leeuwenhoek—born on this day in 1632—was the first person to observe microscopic life and record his observations. Set up several microscope stations for viewing commercial slides—or prepare your own slides from everyday materials such as a drop of water, a scrap of fabric, a small piece of paper, or a human hair. Have students make sketches of what they see, as Leeuwenhoek did.

25—Pablo Picasso's Birthday

The most famous painter of the 20th century—Pablo Ruiz Picasso—was born on this day in 1881. Share Picasso's abstract style of cubism through photographs of his works. Use the following books:
- *I Spy: An Alphabet In Art* by Lucy Micklethwait (Greenwillow Books)
- *Picture This: A First Introduction To Paintings* by Felicity Woolf (Doubleday)
- *Pablo Picasso* by Ibi Lepscky (Barron's Educational Series, Inc.)

After sharing the books, let each student pick up a paintbrush and create a cubed-and-triangled masterpiece!

26—Make A Difference Day

Encourage your students to join the half million people nationwide who will participate in Make A Difference Day. This is a national day of community service sponsored by *USA Weekend*—a supplement to over 400 Sunday newspapers. Give each student an index card on which to list three things he and his family could do to make his community a better place to live. Ask the students to take their cards home and encourage their families to do their parts in making a difference.

1. Help at the Soup Kitchen.
2. Pick up litter.
3. Recycle our newspapers.

31—Mount Rushmore Completed

After 14 years of work, the Mount Rushmore National Memorial was completed on this date in 1941. It contains the heads-only sculptures of four presidents: George Washington, Thomas Jefferson, Abraham Lincoln, and Theodore Roosevelt. Ask each student to draw a large mountain; then have her sketch and label the heads of four modern leaders that she thinks are worthy of such distinction.

Teacher's October Resource Calendar
A Handy List Of Special Days

October comes from the Latin word *octo,* meaning "eighth," and was the eighth month in the Roman calendar.

3 East and West Germany reunited on this day in 1990.

5 Robert Goddard—ridiculed for his rocket-traveling dreams and later known as the "father of the space age"—was born on this day in 1882.

9 The International Association For Criminal Identification, or the Fingerprint Society, was established on this day in 1915.

13 On this day in 1792, the cornerstone of the building that symbolizes the presidency—the White House—was laid.

14 On this day in 1947, Chuck Yeager flew faster than the speed of sound while test-piloting an XS-1 aircraft.

17 An earthquake registering 7.1 on the Richter scale—and seen on national television due to the World Series coverage—hit the San Francisco Bay area on this day in 1989.

18 Alaska Day celebrates the 1867 transfer of Alaska from Russian to U.S. control.

19 The woman who earned the American record for climbing the highest mountain in the Western Hemisphere—Annie S. Peck—was born on this day in 1850.

21 Alfred Nobel, who established the Nobel prizes, was born on this day in 1833. A manufacturer of explosives, he hoped to encourage the peaceful use of science and technology.

23 Traditionally, swallows depart for the winter from the old mission of San Juan Capistrano, California, on this day.

26 This day in 1825 marked the official opening of the Erie Canal—the first major U.S. man-made waterway.

27 The first of the "Federalist" papers, supporting the adoption of the U.S. Constitution and a federal form of government, were first published in a New York City newspaper on this day in 1787.

28 The man who developed the polio vaccine—Jonas Salk—was born on this day in 1914. Before his death in 1995, he worked on AIDS research.

31 National Magic Day is observed on this day to commemorate Harry Houdini's death in 1926.

October Clip Art
Use on the following items:

- letters to parents
- games
- nametags

- notes to students
- homework assignments
- newsletters

- awards
- learning centers
- bulletin boards

CLASSROOM TIMES

Teacher: _____   Date: _____

OCTOBER

Highlights

Don't Forget!

Hats Off To...

Special Events

Help Wanted

FREE-TIME FUN for October!

Tackle these 20 terrific tasks when you finish your work.

Monday	Tuesday	Wednesday	Thursday	Friday
Fire Prevention Week is in October. Draw a fire escape plan for your house.	Name a bulb that can be eaten.	What's the difference between a *deciduous tree* and an *evergreen?*	What is the total number of legs on four chickens, three cows, and five ducks?	Make a list of ten creative ways you could use a paper clip.
Create a number pattern for this rule: multiply by 3, subtract 2.	Without looking at them, draw a circle to represent each of these coins: nickel, dime, penny, quarter.	Explain why a square is a rectangle.	How old are you in months and days?	Make a list of ten cereal names. Suggest three new ones.
If you could communicate on-line with any of the world's leaders, whom would you choose? Why?	October is National Pizza Month. List the toppings you'd use to create a Halloween pizza.	October 12 is International Moment Of Frustration Scream Day. List five ways you deal with frustration.	Describe the last time you played in a big pile of leaves.	Use the following fall color words in the same sentence: *red, yellow, orange, brown.*
Seven letters spell *October.* List seven-letter words associated with this month. (Ex.: *harvest*)	Squirrels busily store nuts for winter at this time of year. What kinds of things do people store?	What's your favorite candy? Describe it. Make three suggestions for improving it.	Make a list of everything that can be done with a pumpkin.	Should the amount of candy eaten at Halloween be limited? Why or why not?

Note To The Teacher: Have each student staple a copy of this page inside a file folder. Direct students to store their completed work inside their folders.

Desktag: Duplicate student copies on construction paper. Have each student personalize and decorate his pattern; then laminate the patterns and use them as desktags during October.

Award: Duplicate multiple copies. Keep them handy at your desk during the month of October. When a student earns an award, write the assignment she is allowed to skip on the appropriate line. Or let the student choose the assignment with your approval.

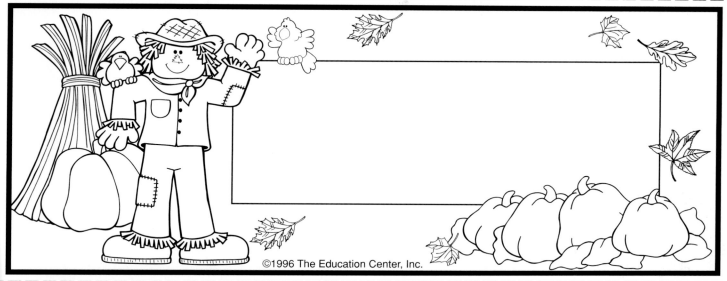

©1996 The Education Center, Inc.

You Can't Disguise Great Work!

I'm so proud of your hard work on _____

This award entitles you to skip the following assignment:

_____

_____

_____

To: _____

From: _____

Date: _____

©1996 The Education Center, Inc. • *OCTOBER* • TEC199

"Howl-oween" Hoedown

"Phan-tastic" Halloween Activities, Projects, And Fun

by Peggy W. Hambright
and Ann Fisher

Bewitching Tales

Turn narrative writing into a spirited event by having students rewrite well-known fairy tales with Halloween themes. Suggest titles like "Snow White And The Seven Ghosts," "The Three Little Monsters," or "The Town Witch And The Country Witch." Have each student fold a 12" x 18" sheet of white paper accordion-style, with one-inch folds; then have him copy his story on the folds (one line per fold). Next have him staple a cut-out head, a pair of arms, and a pair of feet to the resulting body as shown. Plan a time for the tales to be shared with a younger class.

Gordon, a groovy green monster, grinned as he greedily gobbled gobs of gooey, green gum.

Ghost Writers

Excite students with some ghostly science that's disguised as magic! Have each student use lemon juice–dampened Q-tips® to write a Halloween tongue twister on white paper. After the papers have dried, have each student hold his paper up to a light to read his message, which has magically turned brown. Explain to students that the lemon juice turned brown because of a chemical change that takes place when the paper is warmed by the light. Lemon juice contains carbon. When it is heated, the heat causes a chemical change that breaks apart the juice and frees the carbon to show its true dark color.

Rib Ticklers

You'll tickle a few funny bones with this writing activity! Assign each student to write an original Halloween riddle or joke on a large bone cutout as shown. Encourage students to use homonyms and/or plays on words. Have students write the answers to their riddles on the backs of their bones; then staple the bones together to make a class book titled " 'Phan-tastically' Funny Bones." Share the book during a class Halloween party. Or have a student read one riddle/joke a day over your school public-address system during the last two weeks of October.

Monster Motel is near which lake?

Lake Eerie.

Look Whoooo's In My Group!

Create a magical moment when you form groups for cooperative activities during the Halloween season. Stamp the backs of index cards (one card per student) with four or five different Halloween stamps (one stamp per card). Distribute the cards to students; then form groups based on the pictures stamped on the cards.

Halloween Mad Lib

During the Halloween season, have fun reviewing nouns, verbs, and adjectives with a Mad Lib activity. Explain to students that a Mad Lib is a sentence into which certain parts of speech have been randomly placed. The results of the random placement can be quite humorous. Give each student a copy of the reproducible on the bottom half of page 19. After students have followed the instructions and filled the blanks in Part One, read Part Two aloud. At each numbered blank, ask a volunteer to insert the matching word that he wrote in Part One. Listen for laughter as students realize how silly words sound when they do not fit the context. As a final step, direct each student to number the back of his reproducible 1–12; then have him write a list of words that *would* make sense within the context of the paragraph. Let students compare their lists.

She woke up in her dishwasher?

Halloween Page Peekers

As Halloween draws near, imagine a mischievous ghost peeking over the page of a student's favorite book as he reads! Give each student a 2 1/2" x 8" rectangle of tagboard, markers, a pair of wiggle eyes, glue, and scissors. Have the student draw and color the face of a Halloween character on the top one-third of his rectangle, adding a pair of wiggle eyes. Then direct the student to cut out around his character's face and then make a cut on the top half of the bookmark as shown. The resulting tab can be slipped over a page to mark the student's place.

Hobgoblin Safety Tips

Involve your class in a campaign to remind younger students of trick-or-treat safety rules—and ingrain the rules in your *own* pupils at the same time. Brainstorm a list of safety reminders with your class. Then have each student devise a creative way to share these tips with or teach these tips to kindergartners or first graders at your school—a skit, a rap or rhyme, a trick-or-treat license, a letter, a puppet show, a recipe for safety, etc. Schedule a time for small groups of students to make their presentations to classes of younger students.

Haunted-House Writing Center

Ghostly ghouls will gradually inhabit a haunted house when students use this free-time writing center! Ask a group of students to draw and cut out a haunted house from a large piece of brown bulletin-board paper. Make sure students draw 6–8 windows on the house. Mount the house on a bulletin board or wall. Then write the following story starters on small ghost cutouts:

- Scary Halloween movies are...
- The best trick I ever played on Halloween was...
- Halloween should/should not be banned because...
- If I could make a magic brew, it would...
- Halloween has been canceled this year because...
- In the year 2025, Halloween will be...
- If I could trick-or-treat on the Internet, I would go to...
- If I could travel back in time to trick-or-treat, I'd go to...

Glue each ghost cutout to a window so that it appears to peek out at students. Duplicate a class supply of the ghost form on page 19 to place at the center. After each student writes on his form, have him cut out the ghost shape and post it near the haunted house. The more students use this haunted center, the spookier the house will become!

Ghost Money

Students can readily tell you how they spend their money. But how might *ghosts* spend their cold hard cash? For a creative-writing activity, challenge each student to think of five ways that a ghost might use money (to pay for howling lessons, to buy an abandoned house to haunt, etc.). Then direct the student to use his ideas to write and illustrate a story about a ghost who wins a sweepstakes. Compile the students' stories into a book titled "I Just Won The 'Boo-blishers' Clearinghouse Sweepstakes!" Place the book in your reading center. Or plan to read aloud several stories a day as time fillers.

Graveyard Epitaphs

Here's a research project that integrates social studies, writing, and art with a Halloween theme. Depending on the units you're currently studying, assign each student a different famous person to research (for example, a famous New World explorer, a famous person in your state's history, a famous author, etc.). After each student has completed her research, explain that an *epitaph* is an inscription written on a tombstone in memory of the person buried there. Give each student a large sheet of gray paper, scissors, and a black marker. After the student has drawn and cut out her paper tombstone, challenge her to label the cutout with a humorous two- or four-line epitaph based on her famous person's achievements. Display the tombstones on a bulletin-board graveyard titled "A Graveyard Of Greats."

The Great Pumpkin Race

Motivate students to do their best during the sometimes distracting season of Halloween with this group incentive. Duplicate one copy of the ghost pattern on page 19 for each group. Label each group's ghost with the names of the group members. Staple a pumpkin cutout for each group along the bottom of a bulletin board; then pin its ghost on top of the pumpkin as shown. Each day that a group displays responsible behavior, turns in homework, or displays any other skill you wish to develop, remove its ghost and place another pumpkin on top of the previous one. Challenge each group to raise its ghost to the top of the bulletin board or even to the ceiling. When a group's ghost reaches this monumental height, surprise its members with a treat or popcorn party.

I'd like to bite into these!

Preserve The Pulp!

Carving jack-o'-lanterns is a tradition at Halloween—but what do you do with the poor pumpkin's insides? Don't throw it away—cook it up with the help of some student-created pumpkin cookbooks! Encourage each student to bring a favorite pumpkin recipe from home. During free time, let a small group of students sort the recipes into categories—puddings, cakes, pies, cookies, sweet breads, soups, snacks, etc. Duplicate the recipes for the students (one complete set per child). Then have each student staple his copies in a folded sheet of construction paper. Provide markers so that students can design their own cookbook covers. Send the cookbooks home for use throughout the upcoming Thanksgiving and Christmas holidays.

Abracadabra Patterns

Create fun, magical patterns with this math activity! Have a group of students help you fill individual Ziploc® bags—one per student—with a pipe cleaner, 24 black tri-beads, and 12 orange tri-beads (tri-beads are available from a craft store). Give each student one of the bags. Challenge the student to determine a repeating pattern that can be made by threading all of the beads onto the pipe cleaner. Be sure to inform students that there is more than one solution to this challenge; then set them loose to start threadin'! *(The following repeating patterns are possible with this set of beads: two black and one orange bead, six black and three orange beads, and 12 black and six orange beads.)*

Scary Words

Challenge students to expand their vocabularies with this Halloween activity. First have students brainstorm a list of "scary" words—words they encounter in spooky stories or scary movies. After you've listed about 15 words on the chalkboard, divide your students into pairs and instruct each pair to write a Halloween story—*without* using any of the words on the board. Challenge students to use dictionaries and thesauruses to find synonyms for the words on the board. After each pair has shared its story with the class, add the new words these students used to a chart. Encourage students to use these new words in other Halloween projects.

Candy-Corn Close-Up

Weave a science-processing skill lesson into the holiday season with this sweet activity. Purchase a large bag of candy corn and give each student a piece. Ask the student to study his piece of candy carefully. What is its shape? Its dimensions? How would you describe its size? What are its colors and how are they arranged? Set a timer for 15 minutes and ask the students to list on paper the candy's characteristics. When time is up, have a volunteer read his list of attributes aloud, one characteristic at a time. As each attribute is read, have students discuss its accuracy. Write each attribute that is accurately supported on a piece of poster board. Have a group of students decorate the chart by gluing leftover candies side by side to make one or more large, 3-D pieces of candy corn!

Candy Corn Attributes

shaped like a triangle
3 colors: white, yellow, orange
3 vertices

Geo-Scarecrows

Call on a scarecrow to shoo away your students' uncertainty about working with geometric shapes! Provide each student with a 9" x 12" sheet of construction paper, construction-paper scraps, scissors, glue, patterns of geometric shapes, cloth scraps, markers, and other art materials. Direct the student to cut a rectangle from a paper scrap and use it to form the trunk of a scarecrow's body. Then have him cut out additional shapes—circles, squares, rectangles, quadrilaterals, semicircles, etc.—to form the rest of the scarecrow's body and clothing. Instruct the student to arrange his pieces on the 9" x 12" paper and then glue them on, one piece at a time. Have the student use markers and other art materials to add details to his scarecrow. Mount the student-made scarecrows on a bulletin board as shown. For a terrific border, see the "Jack-O'-Lantern Leaves" activity that follows.

Jack-O'-Lantern Leaves

For an eye-catching border for any October bulletin board, give each student a leaf pattern and one sheet each of brown and orange construction paper. Ask the student to trace and cut out one orange and one brown leaf. Direct him to trim the brown leaf so that it is smaller than the orange leaf; then have him draw a jack-o'-lantern face—eyes, eyebrows, nose, and mouth—on the brown leaf and cut out each part. After the student glues the brown leaf on top of the orange leaf, have him use crayons or markers to add details. Post the leaves around the edges of a bulletin board for a nifty border.

A Decidedly Different Center

When your students get a case of I've-finished-all-my-work-and-don't-have-anything-to-do-itis, what are you going to do? Send them to Frank's Free-Time Fun Center! Enlarge, color, and cut out the Frankenstein character shown. Mount five poster-board pockets on a bulletin board with the character. Number four of the pockets; then fill each with one of the reproducibles on pages 20–23. Fill the fifth pocket with answer keys. Then get ready to do-si-do!

Swing your partner and do-si-do;
Choose a number and off you go
With a free-time activity that's lots of fun!
Before you know it, you'll be done!

FRANK'S FREE-TIME FUN CENTER

1 2 3 4

ANSWER KEYS

Sammy's Spooky Snacks

Terrific Treat Bags

Get your students ready for a howling good Halloween by making terrific 3-D treat bags! Give each student a choice of making a three-dimensional spider, witch, or ghost.

To make a spider: Cut four black pipe cleaners in half. Glue the eight halves to a black pom-pom. Then glue wiggle eyes to the spider as a finishing touch.

To make a witch: Glue wiggle eyes and a construction-paper nose, mouth, hat, and hair to a green pom-pom. Add pipe-cleaner arms and legs to a construction-paper or fabric dress cutout.

To make a ghost: Insert a cotton ball into a single white tissue, tie it with white thread to make a ghost, and then glue on wiggle eyes.

Have each student glue his project to a small paper bag. Provide black markers so the student can write a message on his bag, such as "Spooky Snacks" or "Ghostly Goodies." See "Ghostly Graphics" on page 18 for a great math follow-up!

R. I. P.

RUN

sprint

scamper

scurry

bolt

dart

R. I. P.

SAY

describe

report

state

declare

express

Put Tired Words To Rest

Very specific and vivid words are needed to describe the spectacular sights and sounds of the Halloween season. So dedicate the month of October to reducing students' use of tired, overused words. As you edit your students' writing, keep a list of the common, unexciting words they use over and over again. Then make a poster-board tombstone for each pair of words you want to target, writing one word on the front and another on the back. Have each student use a thesaurus to find synonyms for each of the common words; then list these synonyms on the appropriate side of each tombstone. Hang the tombstones from the ceiling. With an upward glance, a student has a ready reference of fully invigorated words to use in his writing!

"Spook-tacular" Symmetry

"Boooo-st" every student's symmetry skills with this fun art activity. Supply each student with one sheet of black construction paper, one sheet of orange tissue paper, scissors, and glue. Direct each student to fold his black paper in half. Then have the student complete these steps:

1. Draw one triangle away from the fold line for the eyes.
2. Draw half of a triangle on the fold line for the nose.
3. Draw half of a mouth on the fold line.
4. Draw half of the pumpkin's outline around the facial features. Don't forget the stem.
5. Draw a frame around the outside edges of the black paper.
6. Draw double lines in the space between the pumpkin outline and the frame to give the effect that the jack-o'-lantern has been "caught" in a spider's web.
7. Keeping the paper folded, cut out the facial features and around the web lines as shown.
8. Unfold the black paper and mount it on orange tissue paper.

Tape the projects to a classroom window for a delightfully eerie sight!

A Math Trick

Stump your students with a math trick that may just drive them batty! Draw four ghost shapes on the chalkboard. Number the ghosts one through four with colored chalk; then use white chalk to add the other numbers to the ghosts as shown. Ask a student to choose a white number written on one of the ghosts. Tell him not to tell you the number he chose but to tell you which ghosts have that number. (For example, if the student chooses the number nine, he would tell his teacher that his number is on ghosts number two, three, and four.) Tell the student that you know the number he chose—even though he hasn't told you. (To figure out the number, add the numbers of the ghosts in which the number appears: 2 + 3 + 4 = 9, which is the number the student chose.) Challenge the class to determine how you did it!

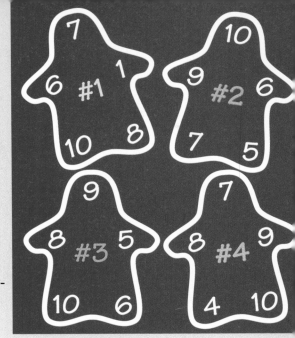

Pumpkin Pals

Use a hands-on art activity as a springboard to a narrative and descriptive writing exercise. Obtain a small or mini-sized pumpkin for each student. Supply each student with markers or acrylic paints, yarn, glue, and other art materials. Give each student time to paint or draw a face on his pumpkin and let it dry. Then have the student glue on yarn hair and a hat. Don't forget to ask the student to name his new pumpkin pal!

To extend the activity, instruct each student to describe his pumpkin pal's personality in a story that tells how he and his orange buddy became such good friends. After the stories have been shared, let each student take his pumpkin pal home to use as a table centerpiece.

Hee-haw
Susie

Ghostly Graphics

Here's an easy way to relate the math curriculum to your class's Halloween party. Request that each student bring in a bag of individually wrapped candies. (Ask parents to provide extra bags for students who are unable to make such a donation.) Have each student set the bag he made in the "Terrific Treat Bags" activity on page 16 on his desk. Allow each student to pass out the candies he brought from home by dropping one piece (or more) into each classmate's bag. Then tell each student to empty the contents of his treat bag onto his desk and sort the candies into groups. Direct each student to construct a bar graph that shows the different classifications of candy in his bag. After the graph is complete, have each student rebag his candy to enjoy during the class Halloween party!

18

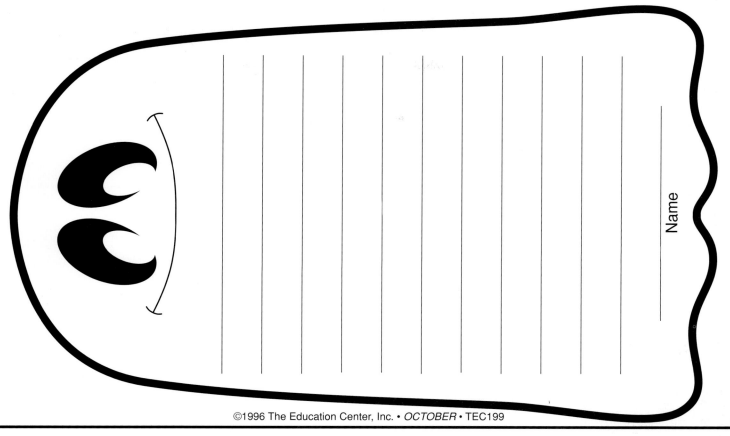

Name

©1996 The Education Center, Inc. • *OCTOBER* • TEC199

Name_____ *Parts of speech; context*

A Parts-Of-Speech Nightmare

To complete this parts-of-speech challenge, cover Part Two with paper. Write a word to fill each blank in Part One. Then uncover Part Two. Read the paragraph, filling in the blanks with the words you wrote in Part One. Sounds pretty silly, right? Now number 1–12 on the back of this page. Write a word that does make sense in each blank.

Part One:

1. _____
   proper noun (place)
2. _____
   plural noun
3. _____
   noun
4. _____
   adjective
5. _____
   adjective
6. _____
   adjective

7. _____
   present-tense action verb
8. _____
   present-tense action verb
9. _____
   present-tense action verb
10. _____
    noun
11. _____
    noun
12. _____
    adjective

Part Two:

Mrs. Frank N. Stein had a nightmare. She dreamed she was in (1)____. She had brought three (2)____ with her, but to her dismay she forgot to bring her (3)____. Two (4)____ jack-o'-lanterns, (5)____ cats, and (6)____ ghosts were also there. The jack-o'-lanterns, cats, and ghosts liked to (7)____ and (8)____ all the time. Mrs. Stein got weary, so she decided it was time to (9)____ home. She woke up in her (10)____ and discovered her (11)____ right where she had left it. It was still (12)____.

©1996 The Education Center, Inc. • *OCTOBER* • TEC199

Note To The Teacher: Use with "Halloween Mad Lib" on page 11.

Costume Combinations

Cosby's Costume Closet has just received a new supply of Halloween costumes. Here are a few of the items for sale:

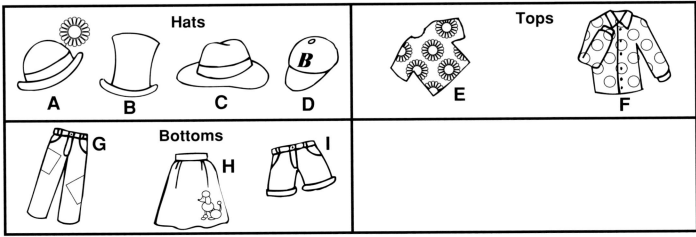

1. Using the letter of each item, list all the different possible combinations of tops and bottoms:

    _____

    How many combinations are there in all? _____

2. Using letters, list all the different possible combinations of hats, tops, and bottoms:

    _____

    _____

    _____

    How many combinations are there in all? _____

3. If two masks were added to the collection above, the number of combinations of hats, tops, bottoms, and masks would (circle one):
    - stay the same
    - double
    - triple

4. A. Look back at number 1. There were ____ choices of tops, ____ choices of bottoms, and ____ combinations in all.
    B. In number 2, there were ___ choices of hats, ___ choices of tops, ___ choices of bottoms, and ___ combinations in all.
    C. In number 3, there were ___ choices of hats, ___ choices of tops, ___ choices of bottoms, ___ choices of masks, and ___ combinations in all.

5. What is the trick or shortcut in finding the number of possible combinations? _____

    _____

6. Add your own drawings of three different pairs of shoes in the empty box above. Now how many different combinations of hats, tops, bottoms, and shoes will there be? _____

    _____

Bonus Box: How many different combinations of two letters are possible using the entire alphabet?

Trick-Or-Treat Trail

Jan and Stan will be trick-or-treating on Halloween night at the eight houses shown below. They live in a very friendly neighborhood, and all the neighbors want to be sure they don't miss the trick-or-treaters. The neighbors have given different bits of information to Jan and Stan to help them plan their route. The neighbors are all very generous and talkative, so Jan and Stan need to allow ten minutes for each stop.

Help Jan and Stan plan their path. Number the houses in the diagram from one to eight in the order they should be visited. Also, write in the name of the person who lives in each house and the time that Jan and Stan will visit.

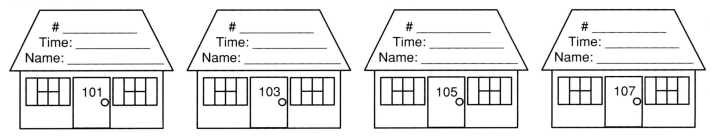

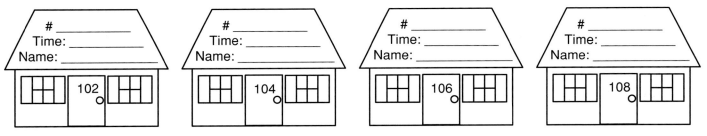

1. Mr. Green at #107 has to leave for the evening at 5:30 P.M.

2. Mr. Black at #102 won't be home until 6:00 P.M.

3. Mrs. Smith wants to be the first to hand out treats when the trick-or-treating begins at 5:00 P.M. She lives two houses west of Mrs. Jones.

4. Ms. Rose, who lives at #103, wants to be visited after Ms. Daisy and before Mr. Brown.

5. The children have been told to go immediately to Mr. White's at #101 after visiting #104.

6. When Jan and Stan are finished at Mr. Green's, they are to go next door to Ms. Daisy's house.

7. Mrs. Jones, who lives across the street from Mr. Green, wants to be visited immediately after Mr. Brown, who lives at #106.

Bonus Box: A man and a woman in the neighborhood above are brother and sister. Both live on the same side of the street, and both have neighbors on each side of them. Who are they?

Word Webs

A few Halloween spiders have been busy spinning unusual webs. Can you complete each web? Place the letters below each web into the blank spaces to spell six common words of five letters each. Each word begins in the center of the web and reads outward. Cross out each letter below the web as you use it. The word PURSE has been completed in the first web as an example.

1.

A I C D E I K L C S̷ T Ʉ

2.

A H R I M N O N Q R S O

3.

A A C E H I L L O P T U

4.

D E G G I L L L N N P S

Bonus Box: How many five-letter words beginning with the letter *H* can you list within a two-minute time limit? Have a classmate keep time for you.

Candy Creation

"Creepy Caramel Cookie Crunchers"— I like it!

The Trick-Or-Treat committee of the Frank N. Stein Candy Factory has just asked *you*, a true candy fanatic, to invent a new candy that will take the nation by storm. This candy must be one that kids will love, parents will buy, and everyone will give away this Halloween. Answer the following questions. Use the back of this sheet if you need more space.

1. What will your new candy be called? _____
   _____

2. Use complete sentences to describe the size, shape, color, texture, and flavor of your new candy. _____
   _____
   _____
   _____
   _____

3. Draw a picture of the candy's wrapper on the back of this paper.

4. Develop a marketing plan. Write a paragraph about how and where your candy will be advertised. _____
   _____
   _____
   _____
   _____
   _____
   _____

5. Next decide how you should be paid. Would you like a *flat rate*—an amount that will be paid to you all at once? If so, how much would you like to be paid and when? Or would you prefer to be paid a *commission*—a certain percentage of the company's profits on the sale of your candy? If so, what percentage would you like to be paid and how often would you like to be paid? Write a one-paragraph proposal to the company's president. Explain how you want to be paid, what you would like to be paid, and when you want to be paid.
   _____
   _____
   _____
   _____
   _____

Bonus Box: On a piece of art paper, design a billboard advertising your new candy.

A Nose For The News

Press

What a scoop!

What better way to observe National Newspaper Week (the second week of October) than by integrating the newspaper into your curriculum! You don't need a press pass to use this bundle of creative, easy-to-do teaching ideas.

by Chris Christensen

The "Marvelous Me" Book

Get to know your students better by having each one use the newspaper to create a "Marvelous Me" book. To make covers for the books, duplicate page 34 on brightly colored paper for each student. To make the books' pages, duplicate an additional supply of page 34 on white paper. Write the topics listed on the left on the blackboard. Have each student select six to eight of the topics; then provide each student with a newspaper and a white copy of page 34 for every topic she plans to include in her book. Direct the student to cut words from the newspaper to construct each topic statement. Then have her glue these words onto the M of a white copy of the pattern. Next have the student cut words to complete each statement and then paste these words onto the E (see the illustration). Have the student repeat this process for the other pages. If desired, have each student glue her photo to the cover on the M or E. When the pages have been completed, have the student cut out the ME cover and each ME page and staple them together to complete her book. Display the books on the "I'm In The News!" bulletin board on page 25.

Sample Topics:
- My name is _____.
  I am _____ years old.
  I have ____ hair and ____ eyes.
  I am in ____ grade.
- I really want to learn about…
- My favorite things are…
- I'd like others to describe me as…
- The kind of weather I am most like is…
- I am thankful for…
- Careers that appeal to me are…
- I want…
- I can…

I'm In The News!

Here's a colorful way to display your students' "Marvelous Me" books (see the activity on page 24). Cover a board with newsprint. Add black and yellow trims so that the yellow peeks out from under the black overlay. Construct the title using black letters. Display the completed "Marvelous Me" books on the board. To create the crowd of children at the bottom, have each student draw, color, and cut out a self-portrait. Staple the self-portraits at the bottom of your board as shown. What a great display for Open House!

Print Collages

The newspaper is chock-full of print types, sizes, designs, and patterns to spark the creativity within each child in your class. Provide students with copies of newspapers. Challenge each student to think of an animal or object such as a kangaroo, car, or city skyline. Instruct the student to sketch a simple outline of his design on lightly colored paper. Then direct him to create a collage by cutting and pasting various newspaper graphics inside his design. Instruct the student to add a title or caption to complete the design.

25

What's Your Opinion About...?

Integrate writing skills with current events by creating this year-round bulletin-board display. Cover a board with sheets from the classified section of the newspaper. Select a topic each week from your local newspaper. Use a wipe-off marker to write the topic on a laminated strip of poster board. Provide each student with a large index card. Instruct the student to write his opinion about the topic on the index card. Post these cards on the board as shown. Each week wipe the topic strip clean; then label it with another topic and have students write new opinion cards.

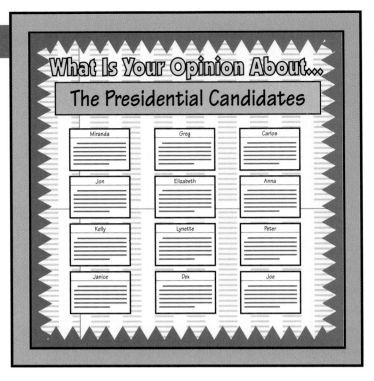

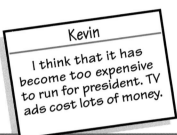

Kevin

I think that it has become too expensive to run for president. TV ads cost lots of money.

The Shopping Spree

Liven up a math lesson by playing The Shopping Spree. Divide your class into pairs or small groups. Provide each group with a copy of the gameboard on page 35, a die, game markers, scissors, glue, paper, and a newspaper section containing advertisements. Have each group set up its gameboard by clipping and gluing one sale item (either its name or its picture) and its price in each square. Then have the team determine the objective for winning its game. For example:

- whoever spends the least
- whoever spends the most
- whoever comes closest to a predetermined sum of money
- whoever does not spend over a predetermined amount

To play have each player, in turn, roll the die and move the number of designated spaces. As each player lands on a square, have him record the name and price of the item in that square on his paper. Then have him keep a running total of his item costs until every player crosses the finish line. The winner is determined according to the objective previously established.

As a variation that provides multiplication practice, have each player roll the die a second time on his turn to determine how many of the item will be purchased.

World-renowned journalist wins again... News at 11.

26

Found...Who Can Find...?

...op critical-thinking and observation skills with this ...a game. Collect a class set of appropriate newspaper ...s that include captions. Cut each photo from its cap-...and glue it to a 5" x 7" index card. Next glue a different ...ption to each card so that no caption matches its photo. ...aminate for reuse and durability if desired.

Distribute one game card to each student. Direct the first student to say, "I found [underline]student describes photo[/underline]. Who can find [underline]student reads caption[/underline]?" Have each student look at her photo to see if it matches the caption that was read. Then have the student with the matching photo repeat the process by saying, "I found [underline]photo description[/underline]. Who can find [underline]read caption[/underline]?" Continue until every student has had a chance to read from her card.

Newly elected state representatives enter the General Assembly today.

"Ad–rithmetic"

Get your students thinking mathematically with newspaper advertisements. Instruct each student to search through the newspaper and select an ad containing the price of an item that costs less than $25.00. Have the student clip the ad and glue it to a piece of paper. On the paper under the ad, have the student write a word problem based on the advertised item's price (see the examples). Let students swap problems with their classmates and solve them. Or place the problems in a basket at your math center for lots of ready-to-go practice.

Examples:
- Show the price by drawing the correct bills and coins.
- What will the change be from a [underline]give a specific amount[/underline] bill?
- How many items can you buy for [underline]give specific amount of money[/underline]?

Petunias 30¢ each or $3.00 a dozen

How many petunias could you buy for $10.00?

If I Could Be...

Imagine being a tennis shoe, a backpack, or a jet ski! Have each student select one picture of an inanimate object from the newspaper. Next have the student write a story from that object's point of view. Instruct the student to answer one or more of the following questions while writing his story:
- What are you and what do you do?
- Where were you purchased?
- Who purchased you?
- Why were you purchased?
- Where did your new owner take you?
- What adventures did you have with your new owner?
- What is the world like from your point of view?

Sneaking Across The U.S.A., Or How To Succeed In "Shoe" Business

Welcome To The World!

Capitalize on your students' love for babies with this creative-writing activity. Tell students that their assignment is to write a letter to a "little one" describing the positive news that occurred around the time that the baby was born. Provide students with recent newspapers to peruse. Then have each child briefly summarize the following in his newborn's letter: two or three memorable news events; a description of the weather; reviews or summaries of two recent movies, books, or television programs; a description of a popular fad (clothing, toys, jewelry, etc.) and its cost; and anything else that the student deems memorable.

Provide students with white paper, blue and pink stamp pads, and teddy-bear stamps. Instruct each child to stamp a border of teddy bears around the perimeter of a sheet of paper; then have him write a final copy of his letter on the paper. Post the finished letters. If any student wants to mail his letter to an actual newborn he knows of, then give him an envelope in which to enclose, address, and mail the precious keepsake.

Dear Salina,
On the day you were born, fireworks lit the sky. It was Independence Day!

Newspaper ABCs

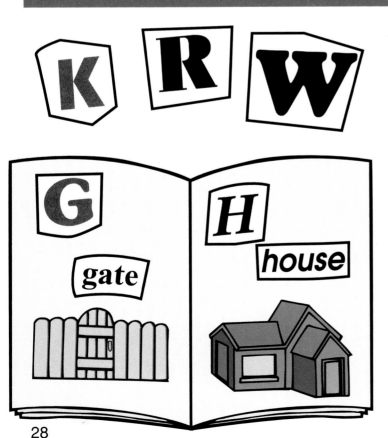

Use the newspaper to connect your students with a class of kindergartners or first graders by having them create mini ABC books. To begin, cut a supply of duplicating paper in half to create 5 1/2" x 8" sheets. Provide each student with 14 of these sheets. Instruct the student to fold each sheet in half to create 28 pages. Then have him staple these pages inside a construction-paper cover. Direct the student to decorate the cover and title page of his book. Then have him scan the newspaper to find one large, uppercase letter for each letter of the alphabet. Have him cut out these letters and paste each one on a separate page in alphabetical sequence. Next have him search the paper again for an easy word—preferably a noun—to go with each letter. (The grocery section of the paper is a good place to look.) After he has glued the word to the page, instruct the student to add an illustration to the page. Set up a time during which each student can present and read his book to a younger student.

Into The Index

Practice essential reading skills by using the newspaper index. Duplicate a copy of a detailed newspaper index for each student (a Sunday copy from a major city works well). Challenge students to tell you which index category they would use to find the answers to questions such as:

- What were the high and low temperatures in Death Valley, CA?
- How many letters to the editor are in today's paper?
- What was the score of your favorite baseball team's game?
- Is there a recipe included in today's paper?
- Where would you go to see the latest hit movie for children?

Extend your lesson by demonstrating how the index saves time. Divide your class into two groups. Give each group several copies of a recent newspaper. Have one group use the index to find the exact answers to specific questions. Meanwhile instruct the other group to browse through the paper to find the answers. Keep track of the time each group spends researching. Which method—using the index or browsing—was more effective?

INDEX

Business	**B4, B7**
Bridge	**D9**
Classified	**E1**
Comics	**D11**
Crossword	**E4, E5**
Editorials	**A8, A9**
Ann Landers	**D9**
Obituaries	**B3**
Television	**D10**
Theaters	**D9**
Weather	**A2**

Graphing The Weather

The newspaper weather page provides excellent data for constructing double-line graphs. Show students how to read the tables listing the high and low temperatures of major world cities. Select a city to use as a model for creating a double-line graph on the overhead or chalkboard. Construct the graph using several days' worth of weather charts about this city.

Next provide each student with graph paper and two weeks' worth of weather pages from the newspaper. Have each student select a city and write its name at the top of the graph paper. Instruct her to fill in the dates on the horizontal axis and the temperature in increments of five degrees on the vertical axis. Finally direct her to plot the daily highs of her city using a red crayon and the daily lows with a blue crayon. Display these graphs on a bulletin board or bind them into a class book.

Washington, DC

OCTOBER

29

Art Museum Opens

The Frazier City Fine Arts Museum opened its doors to the ████ yesterday at noon, amid the cheers of a crowd of ██ 1,000 people. The museum building was built in a record 11 ████ in an effort to open before the city's annual arts festival. ████ Richard Gaines started the ceremonies with a speech to welcome the ████ who braved the cold.

11 months?

Help your students with their comprehension of news articles by using the cloze procedure. Provide each student with two copies of a brief newspaper article (a different article per child). Instruct each student to use a black felt-tipped pen or crayon to "black out" every 12th word on *one* of his copies. Have him exchange his marked article with that of another student's. (Make sure that these two students don't have the same article.) Instruct them to read each other's article and see if they can identify and insert the missing words using only context clues. Have each student use his unmarked copy of the article to check his partner's comprehension. Allow students to substitute words for the original text as long as they make sense.

Sports Jargon

Do your students use the same old words over and over? Turn to the sports section of the newspaper to find some inspiring synonyms. Divide the class into small groups. Provide each group with a 9" x 12" sheet of white paper and a copy of the sports section of the newspaper. Instruct each group to fold the sheet into eight sections. Then have each group copy one of the following words at the top of each section: *win, throw, jump, lose, run, swing, hit,* and *play.* Have each group scan the sports articles to find synonyms for each word; then have students cut and glue these alternatives in the appropriate sections of their sheet. Display the finished products in the room for student viewing and use.

The News Snoop Game

Encourage students to dig into the daily news by having each child make a newspaper game for a fellow classmate. Divide your class into pairs; then have each student follow these easy steps to create a game for his partner:

1. Locate a news article that appeals to you.
2. Clip and glue this article to a piece of paper.
3. Below the article or on the back of the paper, write a list of five challenges based on the article to be completed by a partner. (See the examples below.)
4. Determine how long you'll give your partner to complete the challenges. Record this time limit on the paper.
5. Give your partner your game card. Keep time while your partner completes your challenges; then switch places and complete your partner's challenges.
6. Whoever correctly completes the most challenges by the end of the time limit wins.

Sample challenges:
- Circle a compound word.
- Highlight the name of the main character each time it appears in the article.
- List three words that are written in plural.
- Draw a box around each contraction used in the article.
- Draw a red circle around all words that show possession by using an apostrophe and an *s*.

1. Find three compound words.
2. Underline a name of a country.
3. Draw a circle around three proper nouns.
4. Draw a box around five possessive nouns.
5. Cross out four contractions.
You have five minutes to complete this challenge.

Press

tic tic
tic tic tic

Lost–And–Found Graphs

I wanna go home!

Appeal to the pet lover in every kid with this creative graphing activity. Provide each student or group with a sheet of graph paper and a copy of the lost-and-found pets section from the classified ads. Have each student or group create a graph based on information from this section. The complexity of the graph can vary from a simple lost-and-found bar graph to a double bar graph that lists the lost and found animals by breed. If the activity extends over a period of weeks, have students graph the quantity of pets lost and found.

As an extension, have students don their "gumshoe hats" and determine if any animals listed in the "lost" section match the pets listed in the "found" section. If students think they've found a match, have them list the data that led them to their conclusion.

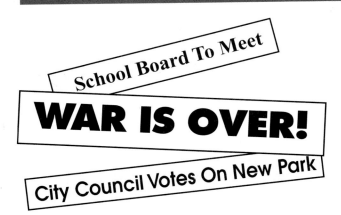

School Board To Meet

WAR IS OVER!

City Council Votes On New Park

Got A Nose For The News?
Then complete this activity!

Explain why you think a newspaper would feature a story about the birth of a white buffalo but not about the birth of a brown buffalo.

sniff sniff sniff

Press

Definition of "news." Hmmm...

Integrate the curriculum and develop independent work habits with these easy-to-make newspaper activity cards. Supply a learning center with copies of newspapers. Duplicate ten copies of the task-card pattern on page 33; then copy each of the following activities on a separate card:

- *Headlines* are the titles given to stories found in a newspaper. Look at the newspaper headlines found in a newspaper at the center. On your paper, briefly explain why you think they are different sizes. Then record what you think is the headline of the most important news story and the headline of a news story that has very little importance.

- Explain why you think a newspaper would feature a story about the birth of a white buffalo but not about the birth of a brown buffalo.

- Novels take a very long time to go from the author's mind to the printed copy. Spelling and punctuation errors are rarely found in novels. Yet you would find these mistakes in your daily newspaper. Briefly explain why you think more mistakes can be found in a daily newspaper than in a novel.

- Write your own definition of *news* on a sheet of paper. Then look in the dictionary for the official meaning. Copy this meaning under your definition. List ways the two meanings are alike and different.

- Think about and list the differences between a newspaper and a magazine.

newspaper	magazine

- List the types of stories you might include in your class or school newspaper if you were the editor.

- Why do you think newspaper publishers sometimes divide their papers into sections with letter names and then page numbers? Write your answer on your paper.

- Why would a newspaper in a large city such as Seattle or Boston have more pages than the newspaper found in a small town? Explain your answer in a paragraph.

- Why would a newspaper report on a public office election and not on an elementary school election? Write your answer on your paper.

- Examine the paper on which your newspaper is printed. Answer these questions on your paper:
    a. Is the paper thick or thin?
    b. Hold one sheet up to the light. Can you see light through it?
    c. Is the paper dyed like construction paper?
    d. Do you think the paper is cheap or expensive? Why?
    e. Why do you think newspaper publishers use this type of paper?

Pattern

Got A Nose For The News?
Then complete this activity!

Pattern
Use with "The 'Marvelous Me' Book" on page 24 and "I'm In The News!" on page 25.

Name(s) _____ *Game: adding and subtracting money*

The Shopping Spree

START

Lose one turn.

SALE!

Receive $20 refund.

Return to Start.

NEW

Pay $50 tax.

Get $100 rebate.

FINISH

A–Hunting You Will Go!

Without careful observation, it is hard to notice the many different things written in the newspaper. Nick Knohitall—cub reporter—amazes his friends with his ability to find lots of hidden things written in the paper. Let's see how well you do!

Directions: Use the newspaper to find words for each category and letter listed on the chart below. When you find a word that starts with one of the letters and also fits in a category, cut it out; then glue it in the appropriate box.

	Person's Name	Plural Word	Business Name	City Or Country Name
N				
E				
W				
S				
P				
A				
P				
E				
R				

Bonus Box: Create a newspaper hunt grid like the one above for a friend. Use four different categories.

Video News

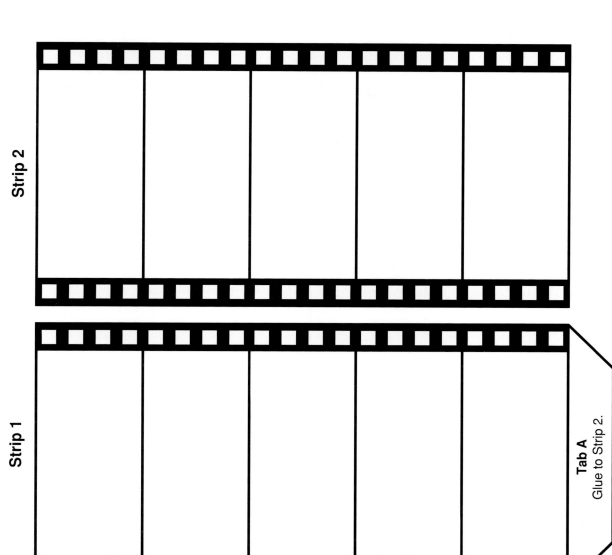

Strip 2

Strip 1

Tab A
Glue to Strip 2.

Nick Knohitall's nose knows news like no one else's. In fact, this cub reporter has decided to work for a local television station to create visual news stories for the station's viewers. Help Nick organize his first TV news story by creating a filmstrip.

Directions: Cut out the two filmstrip pieces. Connect them by gluing Tab A under the top end of Strip 2. Look in the paper for a news story that interests you. Pick out the main ideas or events of the article. Illustrate these main ideas in sequence on the frames of the filmstrip to create a visual news story.

Bonus Box: Compare your filmstrip with the filmstrip of someone who also illustrated the same story. Did both of you select the same ideas to illustrate?

Note To The Teacher: Provide each student with scissors, glue, and a newspaper.

Getting To Know My State

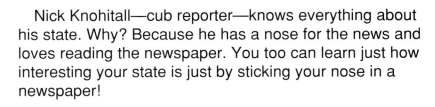

Nick Knohitall—cub reporter—knows everything about his state. Why? Because he has a nose for the news and loves reading the newspaper. You too can learn just how interesting your state is just by sticking your nose in a newspaper!

Directions: Read your newspaper to find information about your state for each topic below. Write the notes in the appropriate boxes. Use the back of this page if you need more space.

Education	Cultural Happenings
State Officials	**State Laws**
Tourist Attractions	**New Growth**

Bonus Box: Choose one of the topics above. Illustrate it on the back of this sheet with a drawing, diagram, or graph.

©1996 The Education Center, Inc. • *OCTOBER* • TEC199

Note To The Teacher: Provide each student with a recent local newspaper.

Use The News

Nick Knohitall—cub reporter—spends his day reading the paper from cover to cover. He knows that a well-written news story answers the six big questions: *Who?, What?, When?, Where?, Why?,* and *How?*

Directions: Search your newspaper to find stories that match the topics below. Then answer the questions that follow.

A Success Story

Who? _____

What? _____

When? _____

Where? _____

Why? _____

How? _____

How do you think this success story could help others? _____

_____

A Story Where A Rule Was Broken

Who? _____

What? _____

When? _____

Where? _____

Why? _____

How? _____

How did breaking this rule affect other people? _____

_____

A Good Citizen

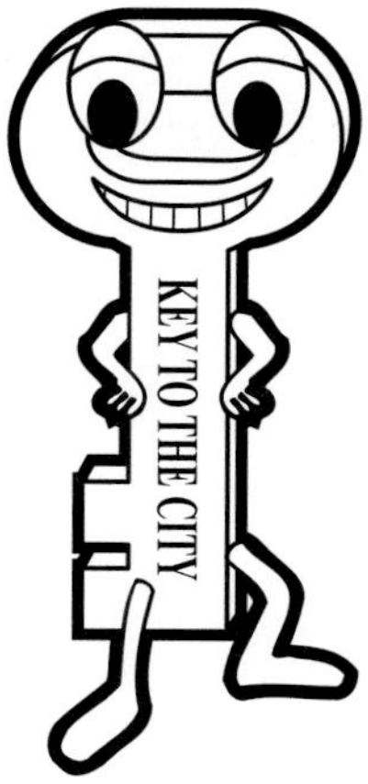

Who? _____

What? _____

When? _____

Where? _____

Why? _____

How? _____

How could you be like this person? _____

_____

Bonus Box: Find either a story about *a discovery* or a story *about a foreign country*. On the back of this sheet, answer the six big questions about the story.

©1996 The Education Center, Inc. • *OCTOBER* • TEC199

Note To The Teacher: Provide each student with a recent newspaper.

A Distant Place Started The Race

Activities For Teaching World Exploration

Hoist your sails, weigh anchor, and sail along with past and present explorers!

by Peggy W. Hambright

Before Setting Sail

Have your students ever thought of exploration as being a race? During the Great Age of European Discovery, a race was exactly what was going on among the kings and queens of Europe—a race to be the first to find a direct sea route to the Indies. Later exploration focused on expanding existing empires to the New World. Modern exploration has concentrated on scientific discovery—but all levels of exploration grow in part from a keen sense of competition among those involved. Allow your students to experience the great exploration race with the following creative activities!

Explorer CDs

Digging for visuals that will help students organize their research about individual explorers? Show students how to make compact discs! Allow each student to choose a name from one of the categories below or from the list of early explorers on page 41. Have each student cut a circle from poster board. Ask the student to put the explorer's name in the disc's center along with a small illustration, and then draw a circle around them. Instruct the student to divide the remaining area into six pie-shaped "tracks"; then have him label and fill the tracks with information as shown. "Advertise" the CDs on a bulletin board titled "Explore These Hot New CDs!"

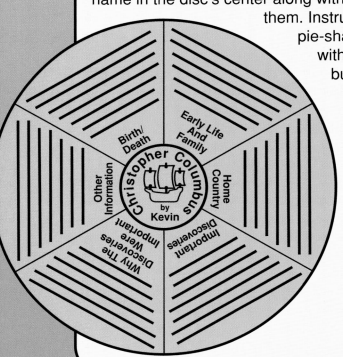

North American Explorers
Samuel de Champlain
William Clark
Henry Hudson
Louis Jolliet
Sieur de La Salle
Meriwether Lewis
Jacques Marquette

Undersea Explorers
William R. Anderson
William Beebe
Jacques-Yves Cousteau
Jacques Piccard
Don Walsh

Polar Explorers
Roald Amundsen
William Baffin
Vitus Bering
Richard E. Byrd
Matthew A. Henson
Sir Edmund Hillary
Sir Robert McClure
Robert E. Peary
Sir James C. Ross
Robert F. Scott

Space Explorers
Neil A. Armstrong
Yuri A. Gagarin
Alexei A. Leonov
Valentina V. Tereshkova
John W. Young

Off And Aweigh!

Launch an explorer unit with a seaworthy bulletin board that has built-in skill practice! Use the list below to assign each student an explorer to research. Then have each student complete the following steps, using the patterns on page 49:

Early Explorers
Leif Ericson
Vasco Núñez de Balboa
John Cabot
Pedro Álvares Cabral
Jacques Cartier
Christopher Columbus
Francisco de Coronado
Hernando Cortés
Vasco Da Gama
Hernando De Soto
Bartolomeu Dias
Sir Francis Drake
Ferdinand Magellan
Francisco Pizarro
Juan Ponce de León
Giovanni da Verrazano
Amerigo Vespucci

1. Fold a sheet of lined paper in half from top to bottom. Cut along the fold to make two halves.
2. Write a brief summary of the explorer's accomplishments vertically on one half sheet.
3. Fold the other piece of paper in half again vertically and cut along the fold. Write your name on one of these pieces and the explorer's name on the other.
4. Punch a hole in the top and bottom of all three pieces.
5. Insert a straw through the holes of each piece of paper; then staple the straws to a boat pattern.
6. Write the explorer's name on the boat.
7. Glue the boat to a blue wave pattern.

Staple the completed boats to a bulletin board. Add an animated wind cloud to start the ships on their way!

Puppet Playlets

Follow a study of explorers with an activity that allows you to discover budding playwrights and set designers. Ask each student to work with a partner and write a short puppet play that shares the accomplishments of a famous explorer. Direct each pair to make the following preparations for performing the playlet:

- To set up a stage, place a piece of cardboard on top of two stacks of books.
- Draw a backdrop of scenery on drawing paper and tape it to the inside of a cardboard box. Position the box behind the stage.
- Make characters from poster board. Dress each one with fabric scraps, crayons, or other materials. (Or students can draw on clothing with crayons.)
- Glue an empty matchbox to the bottom of each character as shown.
- Tape a nail to the bottom of each matchbox.
- Tie a magnet to the end of a yardstick with string.
- Practice moving a character by holding the yardstick magnet underneath the stage where it cannot be seen.

Have students perform their playlets at an Open House or a gathering of other classes.

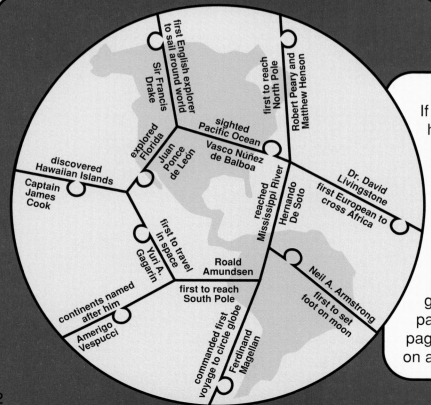

Piece By Piece

If students are "puzzled" by exploration, help them "piece" it together! Duplicate page 50 on white construction paper for each child. Have each student cut out the puzzle pieces and connect them to make a globe. The trick is to connect the pieces so that each explorer is adjacent to his accomplishment. After the student has pieced his puzzle together correctly, have him glue it to another sheet of construction paper and complete the instructions on page 50. Display the completed puzzles on a wall or bulletin board.

Ready-To-Make Compasses

What explorer in his right mind would set sail without a compass? Have students make their own compasses with bar magnets and easy-to-find items from home. Secure the needed materials for each student or group of students: a bar magnet, a needle, a two-inch circle of Styrofoam®, tape, a toothpick, modeling clay, a red marker, a plastic container large enough for the two-inch circle to fit inside, and water. Have each student follow these steps:

1. Position a glob of clay on the bottom of the inside of the container.
2. Stand a toothpick upright in the clay.
3. Stroke one end of the magnet along the needle 30 times in the same direction; then tape the needle onto the Styrofoam® circle.
4. Rest the circle on the toothpick; then fill the container with water.

When water reaches the circle, the circle will float and turn. Explain that the needle will point toward Earth's North Pole when it stops moving. Have the student mark this end by drawing a red triangle on the circle.

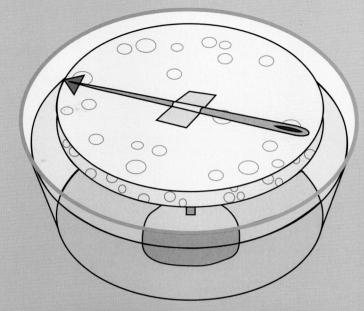

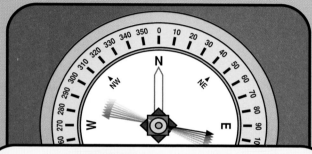

Staying The Course

Expect interesting reactions with this compass activity! Have students conduct the reproducible experiment on page 51 to find out why steering adjustments need to be made when sailing close to Earth's North Pole. Divide students into groups of two, provide copies of the experiment and the needed materials, and get ready for surprised comments.

Finding Your Way

Panic? Fear? Confusion? What does one do when lost? Help your students have an explorer's assurance of knowing which way is north, south, and everything in between. First remind students that the sun rises in the east and sets in the west; therefore, to the left of east is north, and opposite north is south. With these facts established, make a large, poster-sized compass rose labeled with cardinal and intermediate directions. Begin the activity by establishing the north direction. Name an object within the room; then ask students to name a different object that is N, S, E, or W (or NE, SE, NW, or SW) of the named object. Use this as a transition activity several times throughout the year to maintain the skill.

"The sun rises in the east. Therefore, this is north."

Land, Ho!

Ask each student to pretend that he is on board a ship sailing westward from Europe about the year 1486 on the eve of the age of discovery. Remind him that at this particular time in history, Europeans knew only about their own continent, part of Asia, and the northern perimeter of Africa. Tell him that most of the world map is blank and that he is about to change all of that. Direct each student to visualize himself in the crow's nest of a ship—sighting an undiscovered land. Have the student draw a map that shows the following information about his newly discovered land:

- its name
- the location of its major landforms and bodies of water
- a map key
- a compass rose

Ask each student to color his map. In addition, have the student write a paragraph describing what he found when he explored his discovery—plants, animals, people, etc. Provide time for students to share their maps and paragraphs.

Little Explorer Books

Capitalize on students' fascination with smaller-than-life objects by incorporating it with the bigger-than-life significance of historic exploration. Have each student either research an explorer's accomplishments or read a biography about an explorer (refer to the lists on pages 40 and 41). Provide a class supply of white duplicating paper. Demonstrate how to fold and cut the paper to make the book as shown below. Have each student fill his tiny book's pages with information about his explorer. Display the completed books on a bulletin board with the caption "Little Books Explore Big Feats!"

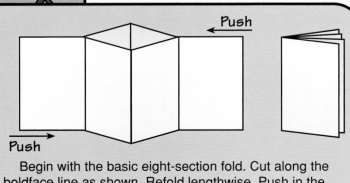

Begin with the basic eight-section fold. Cut along the boldface line as shown. Refold lengthwise. Push in the outer sides toward the center. Fold and close the book.

Explorer ABCs

Inquiring minds want to know more about everything—so provide a forum for expanding students' vocabulary during your exploration study. As research is being done, ask that each student keep a list of new words—one for each letter of the alphabet—and their definitions. Have the student write his words on a poster divided into sections as shown. Then instruct him to make a dictionary of his new words, challenging him to include phonetic spellings, parts of speech, and sample sentences. Display the posters and dictionaries along with other explorer-unit projects.

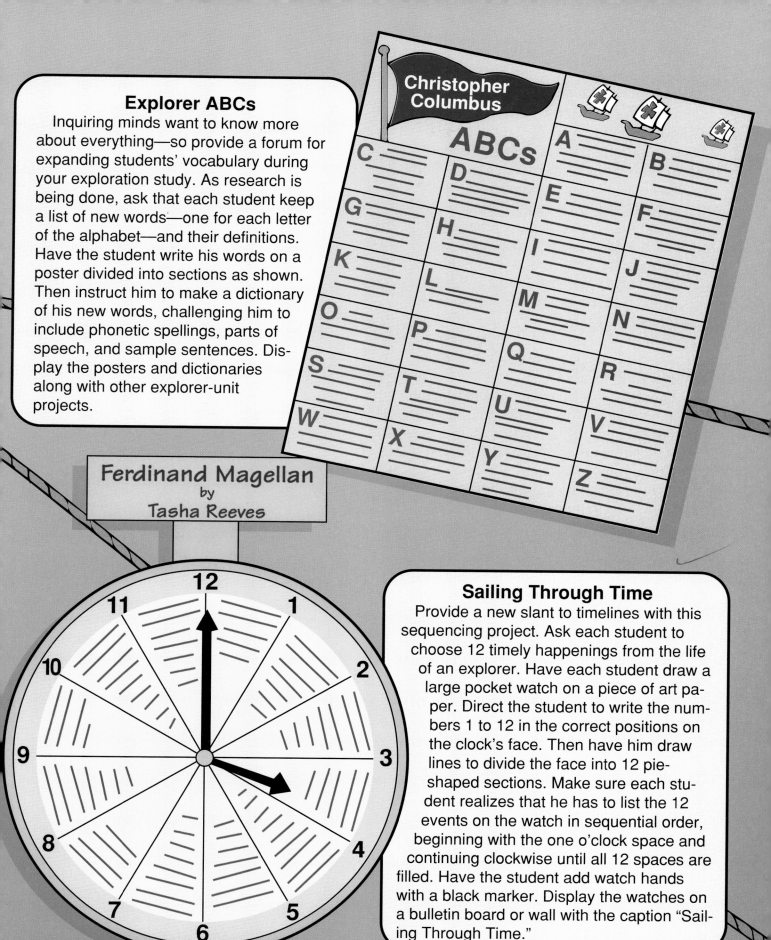

Christopher Columbus

ABCs

A B C D E F G H I J K L M N O P Q R S T U V W X Y Z

Ferdinand Magellan
by
Tasha Reeves

Sailing Through Time

Provide a new slant to timelines with this sequencing project. Ask each student to choose 12 timely happenings from the life of an explorer. Have each student draw a large pocket watch on a piece of art paper. Direct the student to write the numbers 1 to 12 in the correct positions on the clock's face. Then have him draw lines to divide the face into 12 pie-shaped sections. Make sure each student realizes that he has to list the 12 events on the watch in sequential order, beginning with the one o'clock space and continuing clockwise until all 12 spaces are filled. Have the student add watch hands with a black marker. Display the watches on a bulletin board or wall with the caption "Sailing Through Time."

Treasure Hunt

Go a-hunting for treasure buried by dastardly pirates with this fun activity! Remind students that the race to colonize the Americas also involved dealing with pirates who stalked gold- and silver-laden Spanish galleons. Divide the class into pairs; then have each pair design a poster-sized, treasure-hunt gameboard. Have the object of the game be to accumulate the most loot—by overtaking treasure-laden ships, digging up buried treasure, or both. Require that each game include a written set of rules and questions that challenge players to use cardinal and intermediate directions, map symbols, a scale of miles, a compass rose, several different landforms, and various bodies of water. Encourage each pair of students to include obstacles to overcome (storms, broken rudders, men overboard, etc.) as well. Laminate the intriguing games, if desired, and then place them in a social studies center.

Treasure-Chest Writing Center

Students will be anxious to try out this writing center as soon as they catch a glimpse of it! First convert an old metal lunchbox into a treasure chest by painting its outside with gold or silver acrylic paint. Glue a remnant of red velvet cloth to the inside of the box. Fill the chest with plastic coins and old costume jewelry. Next mount the six activity cards from page 52 onto colored paper, laminating them if desired. Cut the cards apart and add them to your treasure chest. Prop the lid of the chest open so that its loot can be seen by all your buccaneers!

Exploring The Future

We all wonder about future exploration and the marvels it will unfold. Allow your students to travel—via their imaginations—into the future with these activities and those on page 48.

Futuristic Colonies

Delve into future exploration with an activity that involves planting a colony on the ocean floor or on another planet. Review with students the hardships endured by early explorers—traveling in difficult circumstances, overcoming diseases, adjusting to different climates, experimenting with new foods, constructing shelter from available resources. Have students form cooperative groups based on their choice of either the ocean floor or another planet. Distribute copies of the chart on page 53. After students have completed the chart, have each group present an oral report on its colony's status. *(See "Bargain Tours" on the next page for a follow-up activity.)*

Future Pioneers

What drives a person to explore the unknown? Whatever the motivation, an explorer must be undaunted by challenges or fear. He must also forge ahead and make adequate plans. Ask your class to brainstorm all the places that could possibly be explored in the future. Then give each student the tasks of planning an expedition and asking for financial backing, like Columbus did. Write the following categories on the chalkboard: personal characteristics of the explorer, education required, equipment/materials needed, weapons needed for protection, types/amount of food, number of people in expedition, anticipated dangers, what you hope to find, length of expedition, cost of expedition. Instruct each student to copy the categories onto paper in columns and fill them in. Then ask that each student write his plan in the form of a presentation addressed to a company he is asking to sponsor his expedition. Plan a time for the presentations to be read before a group of students posing as a company's board of directors.

Bargain Tours

Extend the "Futuristic Colonies" activity on page 47 by having each student design a travel brochure to promote a tour of his colony. Require each student to:
- include three differently priced tours—a budget weekend tour; a four-day, three-night economy tour; and a luxurious, weeklong deluxe tour
- itemize the costs associated with each tour
- provide illustrated details concerning what is included with each tour, such as modes of travel, any included meals, and what tourists will see and do

Then explain the layout of the brochure:
- Front: Show the colony's name and illustrate its best tourist sights.
- Three inside panels: Give each plan's details (one panel per plan).
- Back of panel three: List available tour dates.
- Back of panel two: Show the name and address of the tour agency. The agency's name should reveal the student's identity in some way, like "Jeffrey's Intergalactic Space Adventures" or "Debbie's Undersea Expeditions."

Display the brochures on a divided bulletin board with the left side captioned "Out-Of-This-World Vacations!" and the right side titled "Depth-Defying Vacations!" To extend this activity, have students complete "Bargain-Tour Math" below.

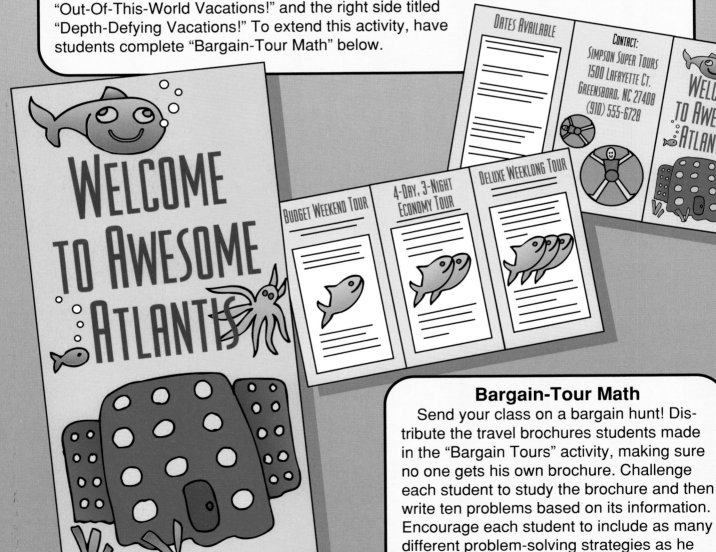

Bargain-Tour Math

Send your class on a bargain hunt! Distribute the travel brochures students made in the "Bargain Tours" activity, making sure no one gets his own brochure. Challenge each student to study the brochure and then write ten problems based on its information. Encourage each student to include as many different problem-solving strategies as he can in designing his problems. Then have each student exchange his set of problems and the brochure with a classmate.

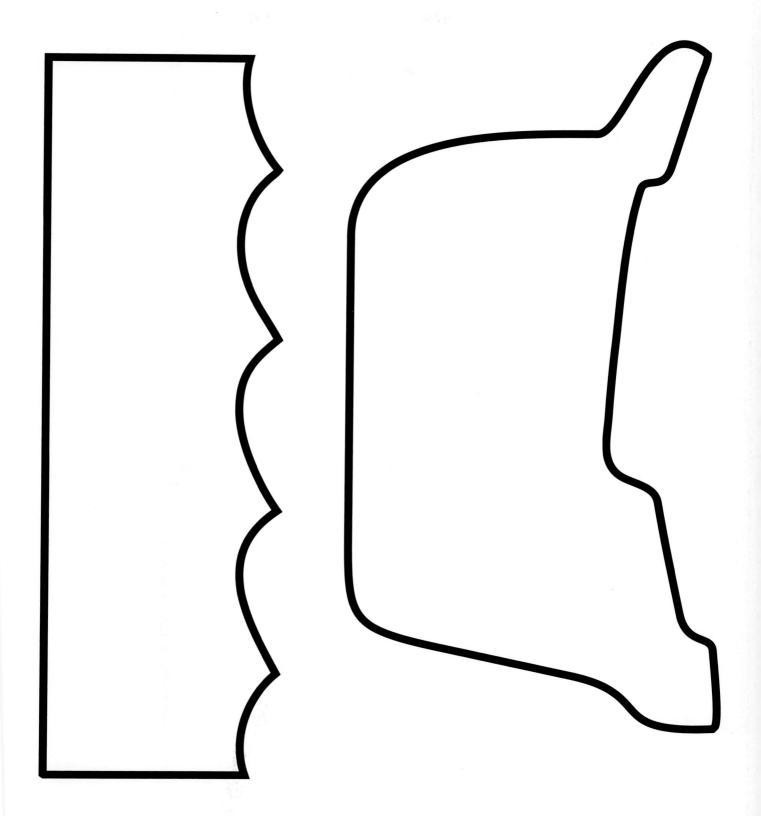

Piece By Piece

Cut out the puzzle pieces and connect them to make a globe. To do this, connect the pieces so that each explorer is beside his accomplishment. When you're finished, glue the puzzle onto a sheet of paper. Draw and color the Western Hemisphere's outline on your puzzle. Use green for land and blue for water.

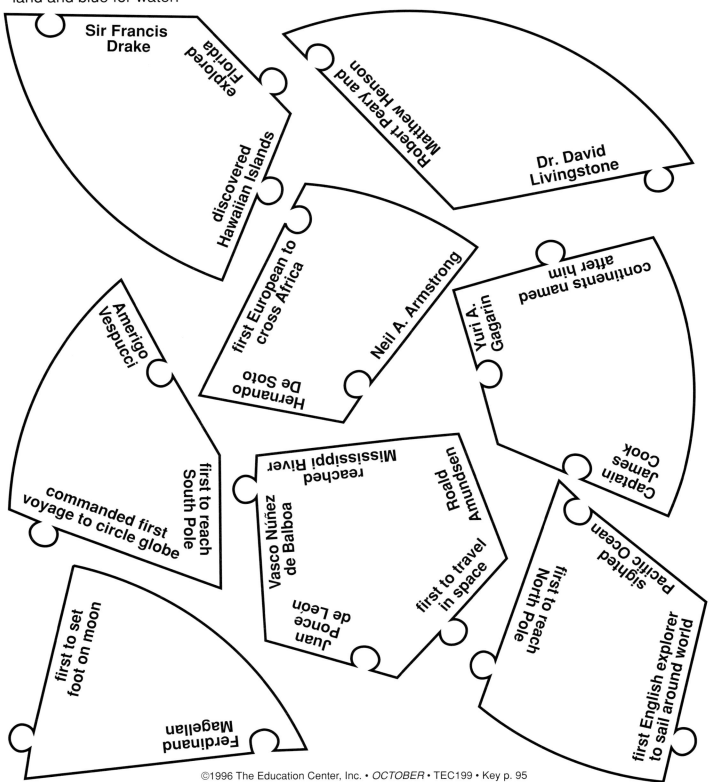

©1996 The Education Center, Inc. • *OCTOBER* • TEC199 • Key p. 95

Note To The Teacher: Use with "Piece By Piece" on page 42.

Name _____

Staying The Course

What happens to a ship's compass the closer it gets to Earth's North Pole? Does it still give an accurate reading for direction? Find out the answers to these questions as you conduct the experiment below.

Materials For Each Group:
compass with degree readings
cm ruler
bar magnet with marked poles
pencil

Directions:
1. Line up the compass so that it points north.
2. Position the magnet 30 cm away from the compass, pointing its north pole toward the north-edged face of the compass.
3. Place the ruler so that its 1-cm end touches the north end of the magnet and its 30-cm end touches the compass as shown in the diagram below.
4. Estimate the degree reading of the compass; record this measurement in the data table.
5. Next move the compass so that it is 29 cm away from the magnet (you can just move the compass atop the ruler); record the number of degrees.
6. Repeat this procedure, moving 1 cm closer each time, until the compass touches the magnet. (You will need to extend the Data Table on the back of this page.)
7. Remove the magnet and observe what happens to the compass.

Data Table

cm Away	Degrees
30	
29	
28	
27	
26	
25	
24	
23	
22	
21	
20	

Extend this table on the back of this page.

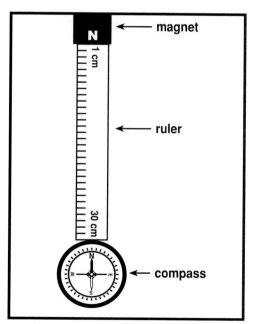

Questions: Write your answers on the back of this paper.
1. What did you notice about the changes that took place from the beginning of the experiment until its conclusion? Why do you suppose that happened?
2. Compare your data with another group's data. Are the readings similar? If not, why do you suppose they differ?
3. What happened to the compass's reading when you removed the magnet? Why?
4. What kind of steering adjustments would a ship's captain need to make as his ship moved closer to the North Pole?

Bonus Box: Use the data from the table to construct a bar graph on a piece of graph paper. Then make some generalizations about the results of the experiment to share with the class.

Note To The Teacher: Use this sheet with "Staying The Course" on page 43.

Activity Cards

Use with "Treasure-Chest Writing Center" on page 46.

1. Rewrite the lyrics to a favorite song so that they reflect an adventure of one of the explorers. Then sing the lyrics as part of a skit that you and some other classmates act out for the class.

   Example: *("Row, Row, Row Your Boat")*
   Sail, sail, sail his ships
   Far across the sea,
   That's what Chris Columbus did,
   His heart all full of glee.

   San Salvador was what he'd found
   And not the Indies shore.
   But he still went down in history
   As part of America's lore!

2. Choose a past or present explorer you would like to meet. List your reasons for wanting to meet this person. Then compose five interview questions you would ask to help you understand the inner drive that compelled him or her to explore.

3. Here is a list of the food aboard Columbus's ships: flour; olive oil; hard, flat baked bread; beans; peas; and salted meat and fish. Write a daily menu for the crew using these foods.

4. In a paragraph, predict what will likely happen in the next 25 years pertaining to exploration. Tell how you think this will affect your life and the lives of others.

5. Write a poem about an explorer using the following formula:
   Line 1—Explorer's name
   Line 2—Two adjectives that describe the explorer, joined by "and" or "but"
   Line 3—A verb and an adverb showing the explorer in action
   Line 4—A simile or metaphor describing the explorer's action in Line 3
   Line 5—An "if only" phrase that expresses a personal wish related to the explorer

   Example:
   Neil Armstrong,
   Excited and hopeful,
   Stepped outside his lunar-landing module
   Like an actor stepping onto the stage.
   If only I could walk on the moon...

6. Pretend you are Columbus. Your men are tired and weary. They have confronted you about turning back because the voyage is taking so long. Write your response to them.

Name(s) _____

Futuristic Colony Planning Chart

Type of colony (ocean or space): _____

Reasons for choosing specific location:

1. _____
2. _____
3. _____

Describe the following:

Landforms:	**Climate:**
Forms of life:	**Possible health problems:**
Forms of shelter:	**Available food:**
Methods of communication (within and outside of colony):	
Types of clothing:	**Transportation:**
Form of government:	**Entertainment:**
Difficulties:	**Other:**

©1996 The Education Center, Inc. • *OCTOBER* • TEC199

Note To The Teacher: Use with "Futuristic Colonies" on page 47.

53

"PURR-FECTLY" POETIC

Celebrate National Poetry Day on October 15 by introducing your students to poetry and their own "purr-fect" potential as poets. Get started with the following creative and easy-to-do ideas. You'll agree that they're the pick of the litter!

by Mary Lou Schosser

danger → dog → bark → run → tree → bird → DINNER!

FREE ASSOCIATION WARM-UP

Flex those creative brain waves with a free-association activity. Call out a word to the class. Instruct each student to write down the first thing that comes to his mind as he hears that word. The response may be another word, a phrase, or a more detailed description. Have students share some of their responses and explain how their thoughts were triggered. Point out that these unique thought patterns are what make us individual thinkers.

Extend this activity by calling out another word. Have each student write the first word that he associates with it, and then use that word to think of a third word, continuing this process to create a unique chain of associations. Have several students share their chains with the class.

THE COLORS OF LIFE

Artists aren't the only ones who know how to express ideas through color. For another free-association activity, have each student write down all of the thoughts that come to her mind when you call out the name of a particular color. Encourage the student to use all five senses—describing what that color looks like, smells like, sounds like, tastes like, and feels like. Next have the student refine her phrases or sentences so that each one describes a different aspect of the color. After the student has organized her phrases into a poem that begins with the name of the color, have her write the poem on a copy of the crayon pattern on page 61. (Duplicate student copies of this pattern on manila or white paper.) Direct the student to complete the pattern by coloring around the poem with the matching color of crayon or marker. Post the cut-out crayons on a bulletin board titled "Color Us Poetic!"

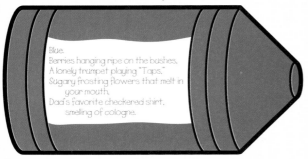

Blue.
Berries hanging ripe on the bushes.
A lonely trumpet playing "Taps."
Sugary frosting flowers that melt in your mouth.
Dad's favorite checkered shirt, smelling of cologne.

A POET TREE

Add a splash of autumn to your classroom by creating this poetry bulletin board. Cover the bottom of your board with green paper for grass and the top with light blue paper for the sky. Add a large, branching tree cut from brown bulletin-board paper. Duplicate the leaf pattern on page 61 onto yellow, red, and orange paper. Give each student a leaf pattern to use for completing one or more of the activities listed below. Display the completed leaves on the tree's branches, falling from the tree, and lying on the grass next to the tree. Add the title "We're Falling For Poetry!"

- Undoubtedly your study of poetry will include a look at the lives and works of famous poets. Keep track of those poets on your bulletin board. Instruct each student to select a different poet to research; then have the student write the poet's name, some brief biographical information, and the title of at least one of the poet's poems on a leaf pattern. Mount the leaves on the display.
- Have each student write an autobiographical poem on a leaf pattern.
- Honor favorite poets by having each student select a favorite poem (or a stanza from the poem) to write on his leaf. Be sure the student includes the poet's name.

A THREE-DIMENSIONAL ALTERNATIVE

As an alternative to the bulletin board shown above, have students display the projects completed in the activities above on a three-dimensional tree. Use a small live or silk tree, or create your own tree. To make a tree, mix plaster of paris in a two-gallon bucket. Before the plaster hardens, prop the base of a large tree branch upright in the bucket. Secure the branch until the plaster hardens (about two days). Place the tree in an attractive planter and cover the base with moss or bark. Have students hang their completed leaf patterns from the branches using string or yarn.

YOU'RE PROBABLY...

Invite students to honor some of their favorite people with this poetry-writing activity. Instruct each student to think of someone he knows well. As the student pictures that person, have him write sentences describing what he thinks his person is doing, saying, wearing, or thinking at that moment. Then direct him to format his sentences into poetry using the sample shown as a guide. Mount each poem on construction paper along with a photo or illustration of the person in the poem.

You're probably...
watching the baseball game
tonight on TV,
holding on to your lucky baseball
as you yell at the ump.
You're probably...
wondering why balls are strikes
and whether or not our team will win.
And I'm thinking of you.

PARTICIPATION POETRY

Everyone contributes to this class poem idea! Cut a three-foot length of bulletin-board paper and draw a five-inch border around all four edges. Write an unfinished phrase at the top of the inside section. Keep the phrase simple, such as "Fall is…," "Love is…," "Science is…," or "Halloween is…." At his desk, have each student write several endings to the phrase. Let students share their endings; then have each student select his favorite to write under the title on the large paper. Next have your students decorate the border around the poem with artwork that illustrates the topic. For example, if the poem starts with "Fall is…," then have each student make a leaf rubbing, cut it out, and glue it to the border. Display the completed class poem in the hall for others to enjoy.

Fall is...

leaf dust in your nose.
raking, raking, raking, and
    raking!
shorter days and longer nights.
hot chocolate burning your
    tongue.
kicking leaves as you walk down
    the sidewalk.
tumbling into a pile of leaves
    with Spot.
football games on Monday
    nights.
time for a new jacket!
relief from summer's heat!

ALPHABET POEMS

Enhance dictionary skills and improve students' vocabulary by creating alphabet poems. Instruct each student to pick a letter of the alphabet; then have him use a dictionary to make a list of nouns, verbs, and adjectives beginning with that letter. Next have him use these words to create sentences that personify the letter by describing it and the things that it does or says (see the sample). Once the student has organized his edited sentences into a poem, have him write a final copy on a sheet of paper. To embellish the poem, have the student glue a spray-painted pasta letter at the beginning of each word that starts with that letter. Mount each poem—along with a large cut-out of its letter—on a bulletin board as shown.

TWO-VOICE POEMS

Instruct each student to select two characters—animate or inanimate—that have something to say to each other. Suggest real-life or make-believe partners such as the sun and the moon, a student and a teacher, a predator and its prey, or an addition and a subtraction problem. As the student writes her poem, have her add emphasis by writing each voice in a different color of pen or with different print on different lines. Finally instruct the student to read her poem with a partner so that the audience will hear the two separate voices.

57

VOCABULARY COUPLETS

Poetry and any topic in your curriculum go hand in hand when you challenge students to create poetic study questions. Instead of having students copy definitions from their science books, add a fun challenge to your vocabulary study by instructing each child to create a *couplet* (a two-line rhyme) using a new vocabulary word. Make a master list of these poetic study aids; then duplicate one for each student to use as a study aid. Afterward have each student assess how the rhymes helped him study the vocabulary words.

A lion is a <u>carnivore</u>—
Eats only meat and then wants more.

Sample 1:
Line 1: two syllables (announcing the topic)
Line 2: four syllables (describing the topic)
Line 3: six syllables (expressing action)
Line 4: eight syllables (expressing feeling)
Line 5: two syllables (the ending—a synonym for the topic)

Sample 2:
Line 1: noun (the topic)
Line 2: four adjectives about the noun
Line 3: two verbs ending in *-ing*
Line 4: a sentence about the noun
Line 5: a synonym for the noun

THEMATIC CINQUAINS

Many poets enjoy the challenge of creating a poetic message within a restricted format. One such format, the *cinquain*, contains five lines. Originally developed by Adelaide Crapsey, the true cinquain counts syllables, not words (see sample 1). It also uses no rhyme. Syllables cannot be split between two lines; however, thoughts or ideas can continue from one line to another. Each cinquain has one main topic. A familiar adaptation of the cinquain calls for different elements of grammar to be used on each line (see sample 2).

Challenge each student to explore a topic of his choice using one of the cinquain formats shown. Or have students write cinquains based on a topic your class is currently studying.

POETIC OBSERVATIONS

The next time your class returns from a field trip or a nature walk, have each student reflect on her experience through poetry. A simple but effective form for reflection is the Japanese poem called a *syntu.* In this five-lined, nonrhyming poem, the writer uses her senses to record observations about an object or event.

Line 1: Use one word to name something.
Line 2: Write an observation about this thing using one of your five senses.
Line 3: Write a feeling about the item named in line 1.
Line 4: Write another observation about the object using a different sense.
Line 5: Write a one-word synonym for the object in line 1.

Have each student write her syntu in the center of a piece of art paper, adding illustrations around the border. If the poems are reflections on a field trip, send them to the host of your outing. If a nature walk prompted the poetry, bind the poems into a class book that includes photographs of sites along your route.

Books.
Heavy and full of knowledge.
They make me feel smart.
Opening them up, they smell dusty and old.
Tales.

Freedom
Right, joyous
Choosing, speaking, believing
Freedom means escaping from slavery
Torturing, limiting, hurting
Lonely, scary
Slavery

GETTING POETRY IN SHAPE

The next time you want your students to explore two opposite concepts, have them create a *diamante* poem. Named for its diamond shape, this seven-line poem follows this pattern:

Line 1: one word
Line 2: two adjectives that describe the word in line 1
Line 3: three words with the *-ing* ending that describe the word in line 1
Line 4: a five-word sentence that begins with the word in line 1 and ends with the word in line 7 (Write this line last.)
Line 5: three words with the *-ing* ending that describe the word in line 7
Line 6: two adjectives that describe the word in line 7
Line 7: an antonym for the word in line 1

I read "The Owl And The Pussycat" and...

How can your students get to know poetry? By reading lots of it, of course. Post a new and different poem on the board or overhead each day during your unit. Instruct each student to consider each poem by responding to one of the following incomplete sentences. Have students write their responses in their journals. At the end of the unit, have students share their responses. Remind students that their responses will be as varied as the poems you present and that differences of opinion are okay.

Possible journal starters
The first thing I thought of when I heard this
    poem was…
This poem made me wonder…
I didn't understand…
I liked how the poet…
This poem made me feel…
My favorite phrase was…
This poem reminded me of…
I wish this poem…

HANGING OUT WITH POETRY

If your students hang out with poetry, it won't be long till they become familiar with *figures of speech.* Provide students with practice in recognizing similes, metaphors, and personification by completing the reproducible on page 62. Then have each student put these figures of speech to use by creating a mobile poem.

To create the mobile, instruct each student to think of an inanimate object. Direct the student to cut out five shapes that represent that object from light-colored paper. On each shape have him write one of the following: the name of the object, a metaphor describing the object, a simile describing the object, a phrase personifying the object, and his name. Have the student use string and tape to connect the cutouts (see the sample). Hang the mobiles from your classroom ceiling.

CLOUDS…

giant ships in the sky

as white and fluffy as cotton balls

swimming their way through a sea of blue

by Jamison

Use with "A Poet Tree" and "A Three-Dimensional Alternative" on page 55.

Use with "The Colors Of Life" on page 54.

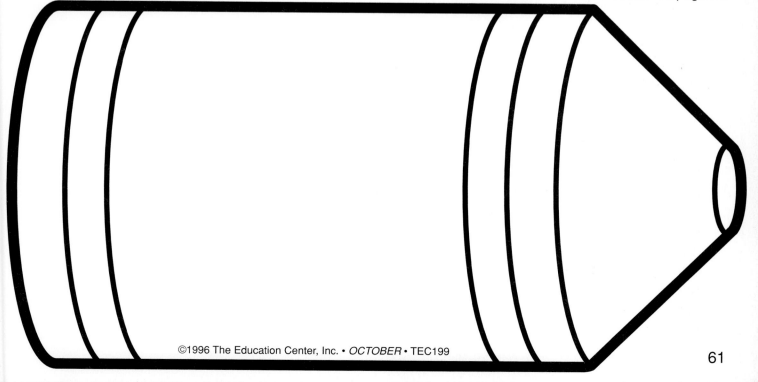

She Was An Ice Cube

Many poets use figures of speech to enrich their poetry. Three common figures of speech are *similes, metaphors,* and *personification.*

A **simile** describes something by saying that it is like another thing. It often uses *like* or *as.* For example: *My face was as red as an apple.*
A **metaphor** describes something by saying that it is another thing (figuratively speaking). For example: *The road is a twisting snake.*
Personification describes a nonhuman object as if it had human characteristics. For example: *The flowers danced in the breeze.*

Directions: Using the definitions above, label each of these sentences with an **S** if it contains a simile, an **M** if it contains a metaphor, or a **P** if it is an example of personification. Underline the figure of speech in each sentence.

_____ 1. The tree branches tapped the windows, asking to be let in.

_____ 2. She was an ice cube after being outside too long.

_____ 3. The car became a bullet as it shot out of the garage.

_____ 4. The small child charged around the store like a bull in a china shop.

_____ 5. The table groaned under the weight of all the food upon it.

_____ 6. When he came in from raking leaves, Sam's nose was like a red cherry.

_____ 7. The spider was a weaver working on his silken web.

_____ 8. The trees looked as tall as New York City skyscrapers.

_____ 9. The waves licked the sandy shores of the beach.

_____10. The stone skipped playfully along the water.

_____11. Janet was as busy as a bee while doing her homework.

_____12. When he became hungry, the baby sounded like a wailing siren.

_____13. The moon was a spotlight shining on the deer in the field.

_____14. Leaves played ring-around-a-rosy in the whirling wind.

_____15. The desert is an oven during the afternoon hours.

Bonus Box: Think of something you saw on the way to school this morning. On the back of this page, write a description of that object using one or more of the figures of speech described above. Then use your description to write a short poem about the object.

Name _____ *Examining a poem*

To Look At A Poem

Select a poem and examine it by answering the questions below. Then copy the poem on another piece of paper and attach it to this sheet.

What is the poem's title? _____

Who is the poem's author? _____

What do you think is the main idea of this poem? _____

_____

_____

What feeling(s) is the poet trying to express in this poem? _____

_____

_____

Are any figures of speech (similes, metaphors, personification, etc.) contained in the poem? If so, write an example: _____

_____

_____

Does the poem use rhyme? If so, write an example: _____

_____

What point of view is presented in the poem? Check one of the choices below:
_____ First person: The writer uses *I* or *me*.
_____ Second person: The writer uses *you*.
_____ Third person: The writer uses *he, she,* or *it*.

What is your favorite part of the poem? _____

_____

Explain why you like that part. _____

_____

Bonus Box: On the back of this page, illustrate what you think of when you read this poem.

©1996 The Education Center, Inc. • *OCTOBER* • TEC199

Computers In The Classroom

Download the following activities into your lesson plans during Computer Learning Month this October or any time of the year!
by Beth Gress

Top This!

Many software skill programs provide the player with a score at the end of a round or game. To keep track of your students' progress on the software you're currently using, duplicate one copy of the "Top This!" score sheet on page 69 for each computer game. Store these sheets on a clipboard near the computer. Each time a student completes a game, have him write his name and score on the appropriate sheet. After every student has had an opportunity to play a game, review that game's score sheet and reward the highest-scoring student with an inexpensive prize. Use the score sheet to identify students who are struggling with a particular skill. Pair each remedial student with an "expert" for some peer tutoring.

"Tech" Terms

Make sure that everyone is on track with computer terminology by requiring that each student pass a computer quiz before being allowed to work individually on the computer. Use the quiz on page 70, or create one of your own using information from your computer's manual. Review "tech" terms periodically by including computer-related words (see the examples in the list below) in your weekly spelling or vocabulary quizzes.

Sample word list:

monitor
central processing unit (CPU)
floppy disk
drive
word processing
mouse
CD-ROM
database
keyboard
printer
input
spreadsheet
font
hardware
software
program

Add-On Story

Use your classroom computer to help students write sensational collaborative stories. To begin, create a word-processing file titled "Add-On Story." Discuss with students the components to include in a collaborative story such as a beginning, a middle, an ending, a problem, and a resolution; then divide your class into pairs. Instruct the first pair to begin the story. Have each of the remaining pairs, in turn, visit the computer and add sentences to the story. Direct the last few pairs to bring the story to a satisfactory ending. For ease in managing this activity, provide guidelines concerning how long each pair should work (for example, require each student to contribute one sentence). Also remind students to write only content that they wouldn't mind having read aloud by the teacher.

Print the first draft and create an overhead transparency. Read the story with the class to check the content. Then print a revised copy and collaboratively proof the paper for errors. Print a final copy; then direct a group of students to illustrate the story, create a cover, and bind the pages to make a class book.

More Add-On Ideas

Continue the class collaboration with the following add-on ideas:

- Have each student enter a favorite recipe from home. Edit, illustrate, print, and bind one copy of the document for each student to present as a holiday gift to someone special.
- Create a class book by having each student contribute one page of autobiographical information. Display this class reference in the library or school office for visitors to peruse. Or keep a copy to familiarize substitute teachers with your students.
- Compose a language review sheet by instructing each student to add one sentence containing grammatical or mechanical errors to a document. Create an answer key by instructing each student to record the corrected sentence on a separate document. Duplicate the review sheet for each student. Post a copy of the answer key for self-checking.
- To review content before a test, have each student contribute one question on the topic to a document. Print and duplicate one copy of the page for each student to use as a study sheet.
- Make a class book titled "Super Science We Love!" Direct each student to type a favorite science experiment that can be completed with materials from home. Allow each student to take the book home and try out some of his classmates' experiments.

Edit This!

Use the power of a computer's memory to create an easy and effective editing activity. Prepare a paragraph (see the example below) for students to edit and correct. Type the paragraph (complete with errors) into a word-processing document and save it under the name "Edit This!" In turn have each student go to the computer, open the document, and make what he feels are the necessary corrections on the paragraph. After he types in his name at the bottom of the document, instruct the student to print a copy of the corrected paragraph. Direct the student to close the document *without saving.* Be sure to keep a back-up copy of your original document in case a student accidentally saves her corrections.

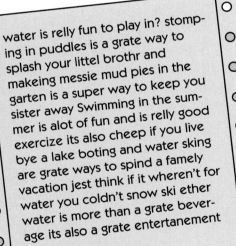

water is relly fun to play in? stomping in puddles is a grate way to splash your littel brothr and makeing messie mud pies in the garten is a super way to keep you sister away Swimming in the summer is alot of fun and is relly good exercize its also cheep if you live bye a lake boting and water sking are grate ways to spind a famely vacation jest think if it wheren't for water you couldn't snow ski ether water is more than a grate beverage its also a grate entertanement

Type your name here:

Student-Of-The-Week Posters

Honor your student of the week—and create an instant display—in one quick trip to the computer. Using a poster-making program like The Print Shop Deluxe® by Brøderbund®, have the student create her own student-of-the-week poster. Display her completed creation on your student-of-the-week bulletin board. Students will look forward to this special treat—and you'll have your student-of-the-week display ready in the push of a button!

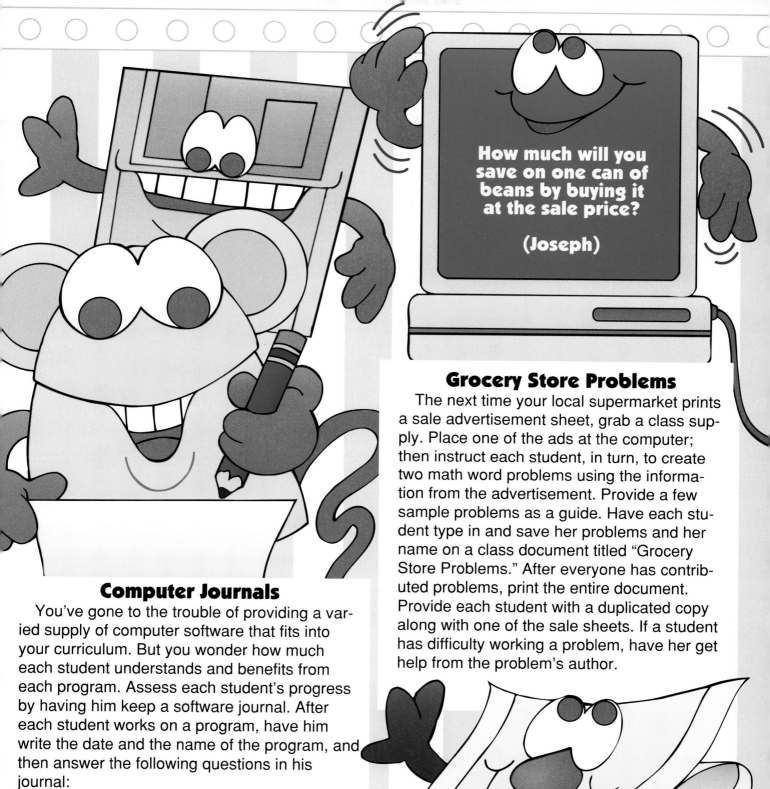

How much will you save on one can of beans by buying it at the sale price?

(Joseph)

Grocery Store Problems

The next time your local supermarket prints a sale advertisement sheet, grab a class supply. Place one of the ads at the computer; then instruct each student, in turn, to create two math word problems using the information from the advertisement. Provide a few sample problems as a guide. Have each student type in and save her problems and her name on a class document titled "Grocery Store Problems." After everyone has contributed problems, print the entire document. Provide each student with a duplicated copy along with one of the sale sheets. If a student has difficulty working a problem, have her get help from the problem's author.

Computer Journals

You've gone to the trouble of providing a varied supply of computer software that fits into your curriculum. But you wonder how much each student understands and benefits from each program. Assess each student's progress by having him keep a software journal. After each student works on a program, have him write the date and the name of the program, and then answer the following questions in his journal:

1. What was your score?
2. What did you like best about the program?
3. What was the hardest part of the program?
4. What, if any, technical difficulties did you have with the program?
5. What did you learn from working with this program?

Kid-Created Databases

Teach students about the usefulness of a database by letting them help you create one for the class. To create a database, you will need an integrated software program (Microsoft® Works by Microsoft® Corporation or ClarisWorks® by Claris Corporation are good choices.) Open a new database and title it "Our Class Book File." Set up the field names you want to include such as *title, author, copyright date, publisher, genre, rating, synopsis,* and *review.* Show students how to open the database, create a new record, and enter data into the fields. Then have each student create a new entry for a book that he's read. Save the document after each entry. When every student has had a turn, allow individuals to browse through the entries to find interesting or recommended books. Also print a copy to post near your class's reading corner. This database will provide you and your students with a handy reference to use throughout the year.

Timesaving Tip

How many times a year do you find yourself writing each student's name—on folders, checklists, workbooks, learning centers cards, or nametags? Save yourself time by creating a database containing only your students' names. Each time you need a class set of names, print them onto press-on labels; then simply peel and go! Or print one copy of the database to use as a checklist for fees, picture money, book numbers, or returned report cards.

Rules For Using "Tech" Tools

Reinforce proper use of hardware and software by having each student create a poster of proper computer use rules. Display the completed posters around the classroom; then have students vote for the best one. Leave it up all year as a handy reminder.

Pam Crane

Top This!

Computer Program: _____

NAME	SCORE

Note To The Teacher: Use with "Top This!" on page 64.

"Tech" Terms

Read each definition below. Match each definition to a computer term by filling in the box with the correct letter. Then label the diagram by writing each letter in the correct bubble.

A — monitor   F — CD-ROM drive
B — CD-ROM   G — keyboard
C — mouse   H — floppy disk
D — disk drive   I — printer
E — CPU   J — mouse pad

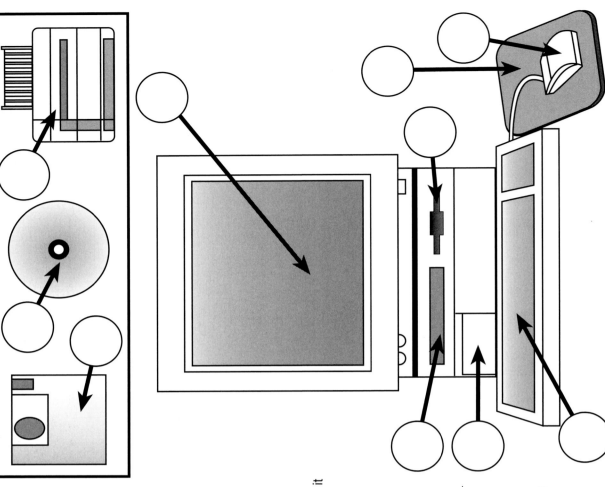

the "brain" of a computer; the part that processes computer information and controls the components of the computer system

the part of the computer that looks like a typewriter and is used to enter information into the computer

a flexible plastic disk (sometimes housed inside a hard plastic cover) that is used to store data or computer instructions

the part of the computer that reads the information from a disk and sends it to the computer's "brain"

a piece of hardware that takes information from the computer and puts it on a sheet of paper

a special surface on which the mouse is placed that provides the friction needed to move the trackball in the mouse

an information-storage device that holds large amounts of computer information, programs, graphics, and sounds

a video screen that displays computer information

a small box with a ball on the bottom and a button on the top; moving this device controls the pointer on the screen

the part of the computer that reads the information from a CD-ROM and sends it to the computer's "brain"

Note To The Teacher: Use with " 'Tech' Terms" on page 64.

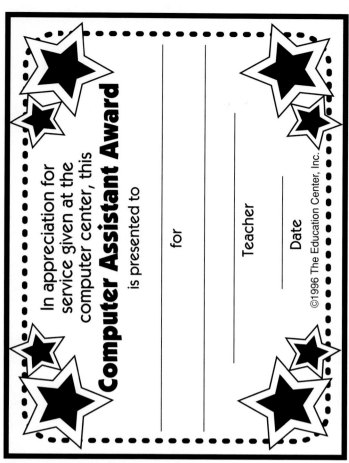

In appreciation for service given at the computer center, this

Computer Assistant Award

is presented to

_____

for _____

_____
Teacher

_____
Date

©1996 The Education Center, Inc.

Computer Pass

given to

_____
(student)

Good for one recess session at the computer center. You may work alone or with a friend on a software program of your choice.

©1996 The Education Center, Inc.

Technology Wizard

_____
(student)

is awarded the title of **Technology Wizard** for outstanding achievement on the following computer exercise:

_____

_____

_____
Date

_____
Teacher

©1996 The Education Center, Inc. • *OCTOBER* • TEC199

The Power Of Peace

Peace—it's an issue that touches every human being and every corner of the globe. United Nations Day is October 24, making this fall month a perfect time to explore the topic of peace and the United Nations's role in establishing it. Use the high-interest activities in the first part of this unit to introduce your students to the United Nations. Then let students take a closer look at the theme of peace with the exciting activities in the second part of the unit.

by Patricia Twohey

A Closer Look At The United Nations

Taking A Seat At The United Nations

The primary aims of the United Nations are to work toward preserving international peace and security, and to promote human rights around the globe. When the United Nations first began in 1945, it had 51 member nations. Since then that number has more than tripled, with 185 member nations in 1995.

In the UN General Assembly, every UN representative has an assigned seat for the year's session. At the beginning of the session, one country's name is drawn at random. That country gets the first front seat. The seating order then follows alphabetically from that country's name. Use this system to arrange your students' desks during your study of the United Nations.

Recipe For Peace

The United Nations was organized to provide nations with a forum to work for world peace and to improve the quality of life for all the world's people. The preamble to the United Nations Charter outlines its basic aims. Acquaint your class with these aims with this tasty demonstration. Have students help you mix together the following ingredients in a huge bowl. Discuss each aim as you add its ingredient to the mix.

AIM	INGREDIENT
To keep the world free of war	3 cups Cheerios®
To assure respect for human rights	3 cups Chex® cereal
To promote social progress and better standards of life	3 cups mini pretzels
To practice tolerance and understanding	3 cups raisins
To live together as good neighbors	3 cups M&M's® candies
To maintain peace	3 cups dried fruit

Mix thoroughly and serve in paper cups.

Where In The World Are Those UN Members?

As of October 1995, there were 185 member nations in the United Nations. Help students become familiar with the range and variety of these countries with the aid of pages 81 and 82. Divide the class into five groups, one for each of the following regions: North America, South America, Africa, Asia and Australia, and Europe. Provide each group with a copy of page 81 and page 82, a set of colored pencils, and a current world map. Instruct groups to find each country listed on these pages on the map; then have them color-code the small marker beside each country's name according to the region in which it's located. After groups have completed this activity, use their colored lists to play Passport To Peace below.

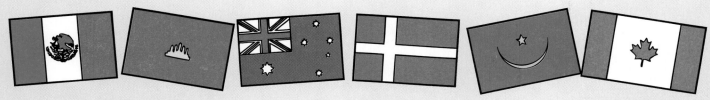

Passport To Peace

This United Nations map skills game is sure to earn your students' stamp of approval! Tape together a copy of page 81 and page 82 to make a gameboard. On a large table place the gameboard, five game pieces, a pair of dice, a colored pencil, a stamp pad, and a stamp. Post a large world map behind the table. Use the same five groups from the previous activity. Each group will need a copy of the "Passport To Peace" pattern on page 84 and its completed copies of pages 81 and 82. Have groups use the rules on the right to play this exciting game:

1. Place each team's game piece above Afghanistan's marker on the gameboard.
2. Have Team #1's Roller roll the dice; then have him move his team's game piece that number of countries on the gameboard. Have him call out the name of the country on which his game piece landed and color in that country's marker on the gameboard.
3. Team #1's Traveler has two minutes to locate that country on the world map. The rest of Team #1 can assist the Traveler, but only by saying, "North," "South," "East," or "West," as he searches the map. Any additional hints cause that team to default.
4. If Team #1 finds the country within the time limit, stamp its passport on the region in which that country is located.
5. Have Team #2 repeat steps 1–4. Continue rotating turns between teams, choosing a new Traveler and Roller at each turn.
6. If a student lands on a country in a region for which his team already has a stamp, he must still locate the country on the map; if he does so, he gets to take another turn until he earns a stamp for an unstamped region or can't correctly locate a country within the time limit. If a team lands on a country that's already been located, the Roller must move the marker to the next available country on the list.
7. The first team to earn all five stamps on its passport is the winner.

(Note: As noted on the answer key on page 96, some of the member nations are considered part of Europe by one source and part of Asia by another source. During play, make allowances when a team lands on one of these countries, stamping the region for which the team needs a stamp.)

- blanket
- jug of water
- bar of soap
- rubbing alcohol
- bandages
- medicine
- matches
- needle
- thread
- canned food

Home Sweet Home?

World Habitat Day—a United Nations–sponsored event held on the first Monday in October—reminds us that many people around the world are without adequate housing. Illustrate the hardships of life without a home with the following activity: Give each cooperative group a large brown paper bag and a piece of paper. Tell each group to imagine that it is a family with no home of its own. Everything the family owns must fit into its paper bag. Ask students to consider what important or necessary items they would want to put into the bag. Allow time for each group to discuss the question; then have the group list its items and staple the list to the outside of the bag. Provide time for groups to share their lists and discuss the choices they made.

The UN provides emergency relief for families who are refugees or who are without homes due to a natural disaster. Challenge your class to help your community's homeless shelters with a similar project. Invite students and their families to donate items for a family-needs kit. Children at homeless centers also appreciate books, small toys, and art supplies, so invite your students to donate items such as these too. Place these child-centered gifts in a bag labeled "Fun Stuff For Kids"; then take the family-needs kits and this bag to a local homeless shelter.

What's For Supper?

The United Nations's Food and Agriculture Organization (FAO) works hard to eliminate hunger and to raise the levels of nutrition and standards of living around the world. October 16, the day the FAO was founded, is World Food Day. Build student awareness of world hunger by examining the nutrition pyramid. After students have grasped the basic building blocks of a balanced diet, ask a nutritionist or doctor to visit your classroom. Have your guest speaker discuss the effects of poor nutrition on health and well-being. Finally have students put their new knowledge about the devastating effects of hunger into action by sponsoring a food drive. On a hallway bulletin board, staple giant, cut-out letters that spell "WE CAN HELP!" With a pencil, divide each letter into 15–25 sections (see the example). Each time a student donates a can of food to the drive, let him place a self-sticking star in a letter's section. When all of the letters' sections have been starred, hold a boxing party during which the canned goods are placed in decorated boxes. Donate the boxes to a local organization that feeds the hungry.

A Closer Look At Peace

Peace Is...

What is peace? Does it make a sound, have a taste, or feel like something familiar? As a class, brainstorm definitions of *peace* and list them on a chart under the title "Peace." Next explain that a *simile* is a comparison between two objects, using words such as *like* or *as* (for example, "The leaves danced like ballerinas."). Give some examples of similes; then challenge students to create similes about peace. Record the students' similes on a new chart titled "Peace Similes." Take the lesson further by explaining that *metaphors* also compare two different things, but without using words such as *like* or *as* (for example, "The leaves were dancing ballerinas."). Give examples; then have students work cooperatively to create metaphors about peace to list on a chart titled "Peace Metaphors." Post the three charts. Instruct each student to write a poem or an essay titled "Peace Is...." Allow the students to draw ideas and phrases from the charts. Display the writings on a light blue paper or cloth banner that you have draped and tacked to a bulletin board or wall as shown.

Conflict On Stage

Conflict isn't just something that happens between world powers—it happens every day in your classroom. Focus on the conflicts that cause peace to be broken in your students' everyday lives by dividing the class into groups of three or four. Have each group identify a situation that involves conflict between children. Have the group prepare and present a skit that dramatizes the conflict and offers a resolution. After each group's skit, discuss with students the conflict and its resolution. Allow other class members to offer different points of view or other possible resolutions. After all of the skits have been presented, have each student write about a conflict he has recently had with a classmate, friend, or family member. Have the student tell whether he thought the resolution was positive or negative, what he would do differently next time, and what advice he would give to someone facing a similar conflict. Let volunteers share their writings.

PEACE IS...

Peace: It's In Your Hands!

Create this eye-catching bulletin board to introduce your unit on peace. Cover a board with yellow background paper. Distribute 6" x 9" sheets of paper in colors that reflect the skin tones of people from around the world. Instruct each student to trace his hand on two or three sheets and then cut out the tracings. Use the hand cutouts to spell "PEACE." Add the title as shown.

Disturbing The Peace

Sounds are all around us. They can be acceptable, annoying, or even dangerous to the listener. Very annoying sounds can even be said to "disturb the peace." Brainstorm a list of everyday noises; then have students categorize them as acceptable, annoying, or dangerous. Next have your students complete Part 1 of the reproducible on page 86. After students have predicted where the given sounds fall on the decibel scale, have them compare the actual answers (see the answer key on page 96) with their predictions. Then have students complete the surveying activity in Part 2 of the reproducible. As a class select three common environmental sounds. Poll students to see if they find these sounds acceptable, annoying, or dangerous. Then have each student interview three people according to the instructions on page 86 to see how each person rates the three sounds. Graph and analyze the results of the surveys. Discuss these questions: "Does 'disturbing the peace' mean the same thing to everyone? Why not?"

The Bigger Picture

What causes peace to be broken in the world? Encourage students to investigate this issue by completing the reproducible activity on page 87. For homework, instruct each student to watch a televised news broadcast, listen to a radio news show, read a news magazine, or search the Internet to discover information about conflicts that are occurring in the world. Instruct the student to record a different conflict each night (starting on a Monday) on his copy of page 87, and then fill in the chart with the required information. Review new conflicts each day, adding them to a master chart in the classroom. In addition, post a large world map. Number the conflicts on the chart; then place a numbered, self-sticking dot on the map to match the conflict to its correct location. As you discuss the efforts being made to resolve each conflict, have students share their ideas on how each problem could be resolved.

Be A Peacemaker

An International Peace Garden celebrating the friendship between the United States and Canada lies on the border between these two countries. It has a formal garden, lakes, nature trails, and a chapel. Create a class peace garden during the month of October by covering a bulletin board with yellow or light blue paper. Place a globe cutout in the center of the board as shown. Have students cut out leaves and stems from green paper, and flower patterns in various colors. Store these patterns near the board. Each time a student performs a kind, "peacemaking" action either at home or school, invite her to record her name and action on a flower pattern. Add each flower—along with a green stem and leaves—to the display until your garden is in full bloom!

OUR PEACE GARDEN

The Signs Of Peaceful Times

Brainstorm famous symbols that have come to signify peace: an olive branch, a white dove, the 1960's dove's foot in a circle, and shaking hands. Give each student two, five-inch paper circles. Instruct her to illustrate a well-known peace symbol on one of the circles and an original peace symbol on the second circle. Draw a large 1960's peace symbol in the center of a bulletin board. Post the conventional and new peace designs on the board as shown.

Don't Break The Peace!

Communication is a key to keeping the peace. Play this game to help students understand the importance of nonverbal communication. Have each group of eight students sit in a circle. Instruct one member of the group—the Peacekeeper—to write the word "Peace" on the board. Instruct each group member to select a different nonverbal gesture such as a wave, wink, nod, silly face, or nose wiggle. Make sure that group members are familiar with each other's signals.

To play, the Peacekeeper acts out a team member's gesture. When that member sees his gesture, he repeats it to show that he has received the message. Then he sends someone else's gesture. Play continues in this fashion. If anyone in the circle talks or fails to receive a message, the Peacekeeper erases one letter from the word "Peace." The game ends when all the letters have been erased.

The United Nations has six official languages including English. The five foreign languages are listed in the chart. For fun, substitute one of the following translations for the word "Peace":

Language	Translation	Pronunciation
Arabic	salaam	*sah-LA-am*
Chinese	hé píng	*huh ping*
French	paix	*pay*
Russian	meer	*meer*
Spanish	paz	*pahs*

What Color Is Peace?

Use the figures of speech that students discussed in the "Peace Is…" activity on page 75 to talk about feelings associated with peace. As a class, discuss which colors best express these feelings. Then give students the opportunity to communicate their personal feelings of peace through painting. Arrange the students' desks into groups. Distribute watercolors, brushes, water containers, and paper to each group. With peaceful music playing in the background, instruct each student to paint a picture that reflects a sense of peace. Afterwards have students share how they interpreted peace through color and line in their compositions.

A Patchwork Of Peace

A unit on the topic of peace is the perfect place for a research center on studying other countries. Post one copy each of pages 81 and 82 at a center, along with a box containing markers or crayons, pinking shears, and a large supply of six-inch construction-paper squares. During free time, a student visiting the center chooses a country to research by writing his initials beside the country's name on the list. After the student has researched his country, he labels a construction-paper square with the name of his country; then he uses the pinking shears to cut around the edges of the square to create a patchwork effect. Finally he illustrates the square with words and pictures about his country. Have the student post his finished patchwork square on a large, empty wall space or bulletin board. Challenge the class to completely cover the space with research squares to create a "patchwork of peace" display. Can your students research *every* UN member nation? You can bet they'll want to try!

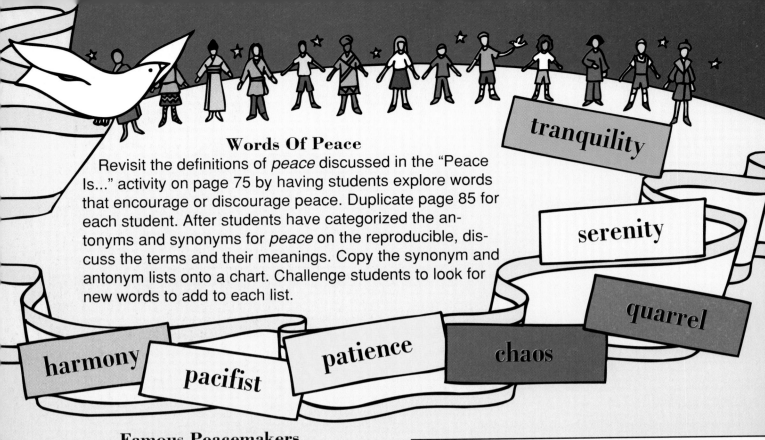

Words Of Peace

Revisit the definitions of *peace* discussed in the "Peace Is..." activity on page 75 by having students explore words that encourage or discourage peace. Duplicate page 85 for each student. After students have categorized the antonyms and synonyms for *peace* on the reproducible, discuss the terms and their meanings. Copy the synonym and antonym lists onto a chart. Challenge students to look for new words to add to each list.

tranquility

serenity

quarrel

harmony

pacifist

patience

chaos

Famous Peacemakers

October 21 is Alfred Nobel's birthday. This Swedish chemist invented dynamite, hoping it would be used in helpful and safe ways. Although it made him rich, Nobel always regretted that his invention caused so much pain and death. Before he died, he set up a fund to award annual prizes in six different fields to people who have made contributions to the "good of humanity." One of these awards is called the Nobel Peace Prize. Some of the individual winners are listed on the right.

Assign each student one of the prizewinners to research. Instruct the student to prepare an oral report that tells the prizewinner's name, his/her country of origin, the date he/she received the prize, why he/she won the prize, and how his/her actions helped the cause of peace. Duplicate the peacemaker pattern on page 84 for each student to fill out and wear on the day of her presentation.

Linus Carl Pauling
Michael J.

Winners Of The Nobel Peace Prize

Shimon Peres	Andrei D. Sakharov
Yitzhak Rabin	Sato Eisaku
Yasir Arafat	Sean MacBride
Frederik Willem de Klerk	Le Duc Tho
Nelson Mandela	Henry A. Kissinger
Mikhail S. Gorbachev	Willy Brandt
Dalai Lama	Norman E. Borlaug
Oscar Arias Sánchez	René Cassin
Elie Wiesel	Martin Luther King, Jr.
Desmond Tutu	Linus Carl Pauling
Lech Walesa	Dag Hammarskjöld
Alfonso García Robles	Albert John Luthuli
Alva Reimer Myrdal	Philip John Noel-Baker
Adolfo Pérez Esquivel	Lester Bowles Pearson
Mother Teresa	George Catlett Marshall
Anwar el-Sadat	Albert Schweitzer
Menachem Begin	Léon Jouhaux
Betty Williams	Ralph Johnson Bunche
Mairead Corrigan	John Boyd Orr

Where In The World?: Part 1

As of October 1995, the United Nations had 185 member nations. Look at a world map to locate all 185 countries listed on this page and page 82. (The date beside each country is the year in which it joined the United Nations.) Use colored pencils and the key below to color-code each country's marker according to the region in which it's located. Then count the countries in each region and record those totals on the blanks in the key.

Key:

GREEN: North America _____   **YELLOW:** Africa _____   **ORANGE:** Europe _____
BLUE: South America _____   **RED:** Asia and Australia _____

▷ Afghanistan, 1946
▷ Albania, 1955
▷ Algeria, 1962
▷ Andorra, 1993
▷ Angola, 1976
▷ Antigua & Barbuda, 1981
▷ Argentina, 1945
▷ Armenia, 1992
▷ Australia, 1945
▷ Austria, 1955
▷ Azerbaijan, 1992
▷ Bahamas, 1973
▷ Bahrain, 1971
▷ Bangladesh, 1974
▷ Barbados, 1966
▷ Belarus, 1945
▷ Belgium, 1945
▷ Belize, 1981
▷ Benin, 1960
▷ Bhutan, 1971
▷ Bolivia, 1945
▷ Bosnia & Herzegovina, 1992
▷ Botswana, 1966
▷ Brazil, 1945
▷ Brunei, 1984
▷ Bulgaria, 1955
▷ Burkina Faso, 1960
▷ Burundi, 1962
▷ Cambodia, 1955
▷ Cameroon, 1960

▷ Canada, 1945
▷ Cape Verde, 1975
▷ Central African Republic, 1960
▷ Chad, 1960
▷ Chile, 1945
▷ China, 1945
▷ Colombia, 1945
▷ Comoros, 1975
▷ Congo, 1960
▷ Costa Rica, 1945
▷ Coté d'Ivoire, 1960
▷ Croatia, 1992
▷ Cuba, 1945
▷ Cyprus, 1960
▷ Czech Republic, 1993
▷ Denmark, 1945
▷ Djibouti, 1977
▷ Dominica, 1978
▷ Dominican Republic, 1945
▷ Ecuador, 1945
▷ Egypt, 1945
▷ El Salvador, 1945
▷ Equatorial Guinea, 1968
▷ Eritrea, 1993
▷ Estonia, 1991
▷ Ethiopia, 1945
▷ Fiji, 1970
▷ Finland, 1955
▷ France, 1945
▷ Gabon, 1960

▷ Gambia, The; 1965
▷ Georgia, 1992
▷ Germany, 1973
▷ Ghana, 1957
▷ Greece, 1945
▷ Grenada, 1974
▷ Guatemala, 1945
▷ Guinea, 1958
▷ Guinea-Bissau, 1974
▷ Guyana, 1966
▷ Haiti, 1945
▷ Honduras, 1945
▷ Hungary, 1955
▷ Iceland, 1946
▷ India, 1945
▷ Indonesia, 1950
▷ Iran, 1945
▷ Iraq, 1945
▷ Ireland, 1955
▷ Israel, 1949
▷ Italy, 1955
▷ Jamaica, 1962
▷ Japan, 1956
▷ Jordan, 1955
▷ Kazakhstan, 1992
▷ Kenya, 1963
▷ Korea, North; 1991
▷ Korea, South; 1991
▷ Kuwait, 1963
▷ Kyrgyzstan, 1992

©1996 The Education Center, Inc. • *OCTOBER* • TEC199 • Key p. 96

Note To The Teacher: Use pages 81 and 82 with "Where In The World Are Those UN Members?" and "Passport To Peace" on page 73, and with "A Patchwork Of Peace" on page 79. Provide each group with colored pencils and a world map, atlas, almanac, or any reference that includes a current world map. For a key that lists the countries by region, see page 96. (*List of UN members accurate as of October 1995.*)

Where In The World?: Part 2

Follow the directions on page 81 to complete this activity.

▷ Laos, 1955
▷ Latvia, 1991
▷ Lebanon, 1945
▷ Lesotho, 1966
▷ Liberia, 1945
▷ Libya, 1955
▷ Liechtenstein, 1990
▷ Lithuania, 1991
▷ Luxembourg, 1945
▷ Macedonia, 1993
▷ Madagascar, 1960
▷ Malawi, 1964
▷ Malaysia, 1957
▷ Maldives, 1965
▷ Mali, 1960
▷ Malta, 1964
▷ Marshall Islands, 1991
▷ Mauritania, 1961
▷ Mauritius, 1968
▷ Mexico, 1945
▷ Micronesia, 1991
▷ Moldova, 1992
▷ Monaco, 1993
▷ Mongolia, 1961
▷ Morocco, 1956
▷ Mozambique, 1975
▷ Myanmar (formerly Burma), 1948
▷ Namibia, 1990
▷ Nepal, 1955
▷ Netherlands, 1945
▷ New Zealand, 1945
▷ Nicaragua, 1945

▷ Niger, 1960
▷ Nigeria, 1960
▷ Norway, 1945
▷ Oman, 1971
▷ Pakistan, 1947
▷ Palau, 1994
▷ Panama, 1945
▷ Papua New Guinea, 1975
▷ Paraguay, 1945
▷ Peru, 1945
▷ Philippines, 1945
▷ Poland, 1945
▷ Portugal, 1955
▷ Qatar, 1971
▷ Romania, 1955
▷ Russian Federation, 1945
▷ Rwanda, 1962
▷ Saint Kitts and Nevis, 1983
▷ Saint Lucia, 1979
▷ Saint Vincent and the Grenadines, 1980
▷ Samoa (Western), 1976
▷ San Marino, 1992
▷ São Tomé and Principe, 1975
▷ Saudi Arabia, 1945
▷ Senegal, 1960
▷ Seychelles, 1976
▷ Sierra Leone, 1961
▷ Singapore, 1965
▷ Slovakia, 1993
▷ Slovenia, 1992
▷ Solomon Islands, 1978
▷ Somalia, 1960

▷ South Africa, 1945
▷ Spain, 1955
▷ Sri Lanka, 1955
▷ Sudan, 1956
▷ Suriname, 1975
▷ Swaziland, 1968
▷ Sweden, 1946
▷ Syria, 1945
▷ Tajikistan, 1992
▷ Tanzania, 1961
▷ Thailand, 1946
▷ Togo, 1960
▷ Trinidad and Tobago, 1962
▷ Tunisia, 1956
▷ Turkey, 1945
▷ Turkmenistan, 1992
▷ Uganda, 1962
▷ Ukraine, 1945
▷ United Arab Emirates, 1971
▷ United Kingdom, 1945
▷ United States of America, 1945
▷ Uruguay, 1945
▷ Uzbekistan, 1992
▷ Vanuatu, 1981
▷ Venezuela, 1945
▷ Vietnam, 1977
▷ Yemen, 1947
▷ Yugoslavia (Serbia-Montenegro), 1945
▷ Zaire, 1960
▷ Zambia, 1964
▷ Zimbabwe, 1980

Note To The Teacher: Use pages 81 and 82 with "Where In The World Are Those UN Members?" and "Passport To Peace" on page 73, and with "A Patchwork Of Peace" on page 79. Provide each group with colored pencils and a world map, atlas, almanac, or any reference that includes a current world map. For a key that lists the countries by region, see page 96. (List of UN members accurate as of October 1995.)

A Place For Peace

Fifteen members of the United Nations General Assembly make up the United Nations Security Council. Ten of the members are elected every two years. The other five members—China, France, the United Kingdom, the Russian Federation, and the United States—are permanent. The job of the UN Security Council is to recognize problems between countries and to take care of them before they get too serious.

Directions:

1. Look in a current almanac to find the population for each country in the chart below. Write the population in standard numerical form in the first box. Then write the word form in the second box. Use the back if you need more space.

China	Standard:	
	Word:	
France	Standard:	
	Word:	
United Kingdom	Standard:	
	Word:	
Russian Federation	Standard:	
	Word:	
U.S.A.	Standard:	
	Word:	

2. What digits are in the following places in these populations?
   China (hundred thousands): _____
   France (ten thousands): _____
   United Kingdom (millions): _____
   Russian Federation (ten millions): _____
   U.S.A. (thousands): _____

3. Round the following populations to the nearest hundred:
   France: _____
   United Kingdom: _____

4. Round the following populations to the nearest thousand:
   U.S.A.: _____
   China: _____

Bonus Box: Use the population figures above to write a word problem on the back of this paper. Solve your problem on a separate sheet of paper. Challenge a classmate to solve your problem.

Note To The Teacher: Provide students with current almanacs. Answers will vary depending on the edition of each almanac. The full name for the United Kingdom is *The United Kingdom of Great Britain and Northern Ireland.*

Patterns
Use with "Famous Peacemakers" on page 80.

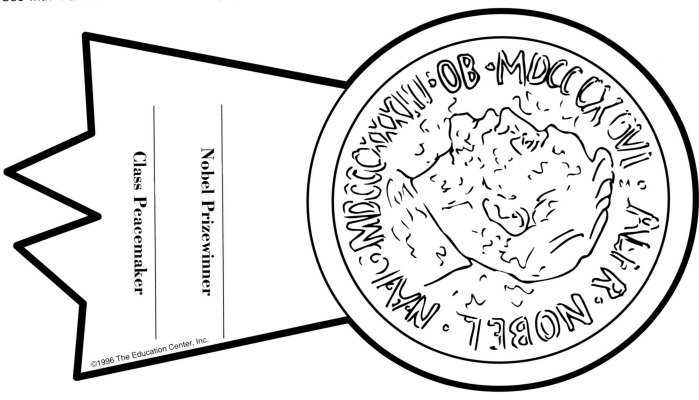

Nobel Prizewinner

Class Peacemaker

©1996 The Education Center, Inc.

Use with "Passport To Peace" on page 73. Have team members write their names on the lines.

PASSPORT
To Peace

Peacekeeping Team

_____
_____
_____
_____
_____

©1996 The Education Center, Inc. • *OCTOBER* • TEC199

Place a stamp on each region for which you correctly locate a country.	Europe
North America	Asia/Australia
South America	Africa

Name _____ *Vocabulary*

Words Of Peace

I. Use a dictionary or thesaurus to write each of the following words in the correct column:

pacifist	quarrel	patience	serenity	animosity
disturbance	cooperative	uncooperative	calm	amicable
discord	agreement	intolerance	truce	strife
justice	impatience	tranquility	war	tolerance
respect	understanding	argument	disrespect	injustice
antagonism	cruelty	chaos	harmony	treaty

**Synonyms For *Peace*
Or Words That Help Peace**

_____
_____
_____
_____
_____
_____
_____
_____
_____
_____
_____
_____
_____
_____

**Antonyms For *Peace*
Or Words That Hurt Peace**

_____
_____
_____
_____
_____
_____
_____
_____
_____
_____
_____
_____
_____
_____

II. Examine the words in the list above. Find a pair of words that share the same base word. Write each word in the pair in one of the first two blanks beside #1. In the third blank, write the prefix and explain its meaning. An example has been done for you. Find two different word pairs for #2 and #3.

Ex. _justice_ — _injustice_ — _in: not, lack of_

1. _____ — _____ — _____

2. _____ — _____ — _____

3. _____ — _____ — _____

III. Select three words from the list at the top of the page. Use each word in a sentence that shows how that word relates to *peace*. Write your sentences on the back of this page.

©1996 The Education Center, Inc. • *OCTOBER* • TEC199 • Key p. 96

Note To The Teacher: Use this page with "Words Of Peace" on page 80. Supply each student or pair of students with a dictionary or a thesaurus.

85

Noisemakers!

Part 1: We hear sounds when vibrations travel through the air to our ears. Scientists measure the intensities of sounds in units called *decibels*. A sound of 0 decibels can just barely be heard. A sound of 120 decibels hurts the ears. The graph on the right lists five sounds. It also shows a decibel scale. Use a pencil to color in a bar that shows how many decibels you think each sound measures.

	-10 0 10 20 30 40 50 60 70 80 90 100 110 120 130 140
whisper	
vacuum cleaner	
car horn	
rock music (close range)	
jet airplane (close range)	

DECIBELS

Part 2: Do all people agree on which noises "disturb the peace"? Find out by surveying three people: a child (age 5–17), an adult (age 18–50), and an older adult (age 51 or older). Write the names and ages of the people below. In the "Sounds" column of the chart, list the three sounds your class has decided to investigate. Ask each person to rate each sound as *acceptable, annoying,* or *dangerous*; then check the correct box in the chart. Be prepared to share your results with the class.

Sounds	Persons	Acceptable	Annoying	Dangerous
#1	A			
	B			
	C			
#2	A			
	B			
	C			
#3	A			
	B			
	C			

Person A: _____ Age: _____
Person B: _____ Age: _____
Person C: _____ Age: _____

Bonus Box: On the back of this page, write a summary of what you discovered about different peoples' opinions about different sounds. Does "disturbing the peace" mean the same thing to everyone?

©1996 The Education Center, Inc. • *OCTOBER* • TEC199 • Key p. 96

Note To The Teacher: Use with "Disturbing The Peace" on page 76.

Name _____

Peace: The BIGGER Picture

Can you find proof that peace is needed in our world? Take this sheet home with you for four nights. Each night gather news information from the television, the radio, magazines, or another source; then list one event that shows conflict in our world in the chart. Complete the rest of the chart for that event. Record information about a different event each night. Be ready to share your findings with the class.

CONFLICT	LOCATION	CAUSE	WHO'S INVOLVED?	EFFORTS TO RESOLVE	MY OPINION

Bonus Box: Choose one of the conflicts listed in your chart. On a piece of art paper, draw a picture or diagram that illustrates that conflict for a person who cannot read English.

©1996 The Education Center, Inc. • *OCTOBER* • TEC199

Note To The Teacher: Use this page with "The Bigger Picture" on page 77.

DIVING INTO THE DICTIONARY

Noah Webster spent 50 years writing his *American Dictionary Of The English Language*. But it doesn't have to take your students that long to discover its treasures! Celebrate Dictionary Day on October 16 (also Noah Webster's birthday) by submerging your class into the following dictionary activities.

by Christine A. Thuman

Dive Into The Dictionary!

etymologist

Rx: One New Word A Day

Increase your students' vocabularies—and their use of the dictionary—by creating a Word-Of-The-Day bulletin board. Decorate a small bulletin board with a cut-out submarine as shown. Have students add paper fish to the display. Each week select a word from a sentence, comic strip, or cartoon; then display a card labeled with the word and a copy of the source on the board. Have each student write a guess about the word's meaning on a slip of paper. Read the guesses aloud; then have students compare them with the actual definition. Challenge each student to use the word correctly during the day. Remove the word card and source at the end of the day; then mount the word along the bulletin board's border to build a visual dictionary of newly learned words.

Final Four

Increase the speed at which your students use the dictionary by playing a fast-paced game of Final Four. Provide each student or student pair with a dictionary. Write a word of seven or more letters on the board; then underline the last four letters of the word. On your mark, have each student look in the dictionary for a new word beginning with those final four letters. When a student has found a word, have one of his classmates verify that it begins with the correct four letters. Award one point to the student who found the new word; then write the new word on the board, underline its last four letters, and continue play. If no word beginning with the final four letters exists, select a new word and begin the game again.

Sporty Respellings

How well do your students use respellings to pronounce new words? Give them plenty of practice by playing Touchdown. Make a supply of football cutouts. On each cutout write the respelling of one dictionary entry word. Number each cutout and make a key on a separate sheet of paper. Place the cutouts in a football helmet or a basket. Label two additional football cutouts "Team A" and "Team B."

Sketch a football field on the chalkboard as shown. Assign each of two teams an end zone; then flip a coin to determine which team goes first. To play, one team member from Team A picks a football from the helmet. If he pronounces the word correctly, he tapes the "Team A" football to the ten-yard line nearest his team's end zone; then another member of Team A takes a turn. If the pronunciation is incorrect, the team fumbles the ball and the opposing team takes a turn, also starting at its end zone. With each correct answer, a team advances its ball ten yards. Each time a team scores a touchdown, it earns six points and play goes to the opposing team. The team scoring the most points wins.

1.

yu̇-'rā-nē-əm

large hairpiece	=	big wig
azure church seat	=	blue pew
angry employer	=	cross boss
sneaky insect	=	sly fly
happier dog	=	merrier terrier

Time To Rhyme

These days you can find a dictionary on just about any subject. One very useful dictionary is a rhyming dictionary. Use it to help your students create *hinky pinkys*—clever synonymic expressions formed by putting two rhyming words together. The first word should be an adjective and the second word should be a noun (for example, *fat cat*). After each child has created a hinky pinky, have him think of a synonym for each word (in this case, *overweight feline*). Direct him to give a partner this second set of words and challenge her to figure out the corresponding hinky pinky.

89

Terminology Tricksters

How convincing are your students when it comes to defining unfamiliar words? Find out by selecting 12 or more unknown words to share with your students. (See the list on page 94 for examples.) Give one word to each pair of students. Instruct each pair to write down the correct definition of its word after checking a dictionary; then have the pair create and write an alternate—but believable—definition. In turn have each pair stand and read its word and both definitions. Challenge the remaining pairs to guess the correct definition. Award a point to each pair that guesses correctly.

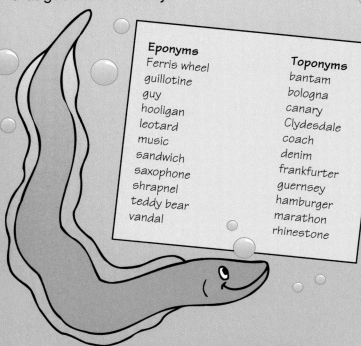

Eponyms
Ferris wheel
guillotine
guy
hooligan
leotard
music
sandwich
saxophone
shrapnel
teddy bear
vandal

Toponyms
bantam
bologna
canary
Clydesdale
coach
denim
frankfurter
guernsey
hamburger
marathon
rhinestone

Don't Take Your Teddy Bear On The Ferris Wheel!

Scholars agree that there are more than 600,000 words in the English language. Where did this many words come from? Some come from things that were named after people. These are known as *eponyms* (from *epi*, meaning "after," and *onyma*, meaning "name"). Others come from things that are named after places, or *toponyms* (from *topos*, meaning "place," and *onyma*, meaning "name"). Challenge students to find the origins of the words on the left using their dictionaries. How many more eponyms and toponyms can they find?

Go To The Head Of The Class!

Many words in our language have multiple meanings. We need to look no further than our own bodies to see examples of this truth. You have a head, but so does a bed. You may think your feet are big, but a mountain has a much bigger foot than you do. Help students explore these varied meanings by drawing a sketch of a human body on the board. Label the body parts as shown in the illustration. Challenge students to find each label in the dictionary and read its definitions. Then have them identify other objects that have the same names as the body's parts. Add their findings to the sketch as shown.

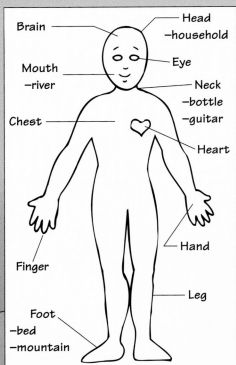

Brain
Mouth
—river
Chest
Finger
Foot
—bed
—mountain
Head
—household
Eye
Neck
—bottle
—guitar
Heart
Hand
Leg

That's Nonsense!

When Lewis Carroll wanted to describe that unique blend of a chuckle and a snort, he created the nonsense word *chortle*. Help students become familiar with the format of a dictionary entry by having them create nonsense words. Give each student a large index card. Instruct her to write the following information on separate lines on the card:

ex•tap•py (ik-'stap-pē)
adj. [extappiest, extappily]
1. extremely happy and excited
The extappy man just won the lottery.

1. The entry word; the phonetic respelling in parentheses, including stresses and syllabication
2. An abbreviation of the word's part of speech; alternate spellings of the word with different endings
3. Definition(s) of the word (which may take more than one line)
4. A sentence using the word
5. An illustration of the word, if possible

Collect the invented words, read them to the class, and then display them on a bulletin board. Appoint a committee to alphabetize the entries and bind them together to create a class dictionary. Challenge students to use their invented words in conversations and in their writing pieces.

Fun With Big Words

What can you do with a *really* big word? Challenge your students with the words listed on page 94 and these activities:

- Say one word aloud. Instruct each student to write the word—guessing at the correct spelling. Have several volunteers write their guesses on the board. Then have each student look up the word to check his guess with the actual spelling.
- Write a big word on the board. Have each student guess the pronunciation and then write a possible definition of the word. Have students share their guesses. Then have them look up the actual pronunciation and definition.
- Give each student a card on which to write a big word, its definition, an illustration, and a sentence using the word. Tape a different card to each student's desk. Each day, rotate the cards to familiarize students with all the new words.

Little Words Mean A Lot!

Anyone who's played a word game or completed a crossword puzzle knows that little words go a long way. Place students in pairs. Have each pair comb the dictionary to discover new three- and four-letter words. Direct the students to keep a record of each word and its definition. Then have each pair use its words to create an original mini crossword puzzle to swap with another pair.

What Is It?

Use a dictionary to find the meanings of these words. Write each word under the proper heading to show if it is a plant ("Grow It"), an animal ("Feed It"), or an article of clothing ("Wear It").

What would you do with each of the following?

acacia	echidna	liana
addax	fichu	monkshood
banyan	forsythia	oryx
bolero	gambadoes	snood
buskins	gaur	ulster
capote	hyssop	urial
chinquapin	ibex	wapiti
citron	jerboa	whin
cloche	jodhpurs	wimple
durra	kudu	zebu

Grow It	Feed It	Wear It

Bonus Box: Define each of the following words on the back of this page: *aphid, auk, azurite, carpal, cicada, curculio, egret, fibula, heron, incus, mica, quartz.* Then classify them into groups according to their common characteristics. Label each group.

Muddled No More

Some words are so similar that they're easy to confuse. Below is a calendar of 20 confounding word pairs. Look up the definitions of each square's words; then fill in the blanks correctly.

mania _____

phobia _____

confidante _____

confident _____

lay _____

lie _____

1
stationary
stationery

Bob's _____ position in front of the television lasted for hours. Therefore, he no longer had time to write a thank-you note on his _____.

2
lay
lie

Stephanie will _____ the book on the table, and then she'll _____ down until she feels better.

3
counsel
consul

The foreign _____ was not eager to give _____ on political matters.

4
adapt
adopt

If that family decides to _____ a baby, they will have to _____ to a very different lifestyle.

5
all ready
already

We had _____ gone shopping for food when Mom came back to say that dinner was _____.

6
complement
compliment

I want to _____ you on a fine meal. The meat and vegetables _____ each other nicely.

7
confidante
confident

José is _____ that Marcia can be trusted as a _____.

8
fatal
fateful

On that _____ day, the race-car driver almost had a _____ accident.

9
set
sit

_____ that pot on the stove before you _____ on the chair.

10
principal
principle

Leave it to our school's _____ to make us aware of that important _____.

11
accept
except

The new store will _____ all coupons _____ those that belong to other stores.

12
raise
raze

In order to _____ money for a new building, the city must first _____ the old building.

13
quiet
quite

Harold is such a _____ guy that most people don't realize that he's _____ funny.

14
affect
effect

The new law will go into _____ immediately. Who knows how it will _____ most people?

15
respectfully
respectively

Brutus behaved _____ in front of the officers, shaking the hands of Mr. Smith, Mrs. Bentley, and Ms. Cannon _____.

16
graceful
gracious

The dance instructor made a _____ comment about the _____ movements of the dancers.

17
capital
capitol

When we visit Raleigh—the _____ of North Carolina—let's be sure to go inside the _____ building.

18
between
among

During the football game, Mark sat _____ Sara and Tyler as all three sat _____ the huge crowd of people.

19
advice
advise

When asked for his _____, the minister was happy to _____ the couple who wanted to get married.

20
mania
phobia

Clara would not take part in the shopping mall _____ because she had a _____ about being in crowded places.

©1996 The Education Center, Inc. • *OCTOBER* • TEC199 • Key p. 96

Note To The Teacher: Duplicate this page for each student or student pair to complete. Or write one word pair and sentence(s) on the board each day for students to complete during their free time.

Don't Let These BIG WORDS Get Away!

abecedarian
abutment
accoutrements
amaranthine
architectural
assuage
bamboozle
bassoon
cacophony
cadence
copacetic
decathlon
dromedary
enunciate
epiphany
eucalyptus
euphoric
exiguous
facsimile
fallacious
fraudulent

garrulous
gyrate
heinous
hyperbole
hypocrite
imbroglio
impervious
impudent
insinuate
jaborandi
jeopardy
kindred
labyrinth
lachrymose
lackadaisical
lethargy
loquacious
luminous
maelstrom
melancholy
menagerie
mesmerize

metropolis
nebulous
noxious
obstinate
obstreperous
orifice
palindrome
pandemonium
perpendicular
phenomenon
polyglot
predicament
quadruped
quandary
recurrence
repudiate
repugnant
resplendent
saponaceous
schism
serpentine
smithereens

soothsayer
spontaneous
spurious
tatterdemalion
termagant
timorous
tintinnabulation
tourniquet
transient
ultimate
universal
vacuous
vagabond
variegated
venomous
vestibule
virtuoso
voracious
woebegone
ziggurat
zucchini

obstreperous

Note To The Teacher: Use this reproducible with "Terminology Tricksters" on page 90 and "Fun With Big Words" on page 91.

Answer Keys

Page 20
1. EG, EH, EI, FG, FH, FI; 6
2. AEG, AEH, AEI, AFG, AFH, AFI, BEG, BEH, BEI, BFG, BFH, BFI, CEG, CEH, CEI, CFG, CFH, CFI, DEG, DEH, DEI, DFG, DFH, DFI; 24
3. double
4. A. 2 tops, 3 bottoms, 6 combinations
   B. 4 hats, 2 tops, 3 bottoms, 24 combinations
   C. 4 hats, 2 tops, 3 bottoms, 2 masks, 48 combinations
5. Multiply the number of choices.
6. 4 x 2 x 3 x 3 = 72

Bonus Box: 676 (26 x 26)

Page 21
House 101—#2, White, 5:10 P.M.
House 102—#8, Black, 6:10 P.M.
House 103—#5, Rose, 5:40 P.M.
House 104—#1, Smith, 5:00 P.M.
House 105—#4, Daisy, 5:30 P.M.
House 106—#6, Brown, 5:50 P.M.
House 107—#3, Green, 5:20 P.M.
House 108—#7, Jones, 6:00 P.M.

Bonus Box: Mrs. Smith and Mr. Brown

Page 22
1. PURSE, PEACH, PICKY, PLATE, PIECE, PANDA
2. EQUAL, ENJOY, ERROR, EIGHT, ENEMY, ERASE
3. STEEP, SALAD, SHELL, SCOOP, SILLY, SPOUT
4. AGAIN, ANGLE, ASIDE, ALONG, AGREE, APPLE

Bonus Box: Answers will vary. Possible answers include *habit, haiku, hairy, handy, happy, harsh, haste, haunt, hazel,* and *heads.*

Page 50
Pieces should fit together to make these matches:
Captain James Cook—discovered Hawaiian Islands
Juan Ponce de León—explored Florida
Sir Francis Drake—first English explorer to sail around world
Vasco Núñez de Balboa—sighted Pacific Ocean
Robert Peary and Matthew Henson—first to reach North Pole
Dr. David Livingstone—first European to cross Africa
Neil A. Armstrong—first to set foot on moon
Hernando De Soto—reached Mississippi River
Ferdinand Magellan—commanded first voyage to circle globe
Amerigo Vespucci—continents named after him
Roald Amundsen—first to reach South Pole
Yuri A. Gagarin—first to travel in space

Page 51
1. As students move the compass closer to the magnet, they should notice that the needle will begin to move farther away from geographic north (depending on the strength of the magnet). Answers to the second question will vary.
2. The strengths of the magnets that are used may produce differences in the data collected by groups. Results may also differ depending on how well groups followed instructions.
3. When the magnet is removed, the compass will return to geographic north because the repelling force has been removed.
4. A compass contains a magnet that points the needle toward the North Pole. Because like poles repel, a compass becomes more useless as a ship sails closer to Earth's North Pole. Steering adjustments are necessary because the distance between magnetic north and true geographic north increases as the North Pole is approached. The captain would need to understand this principle in order to make adjustments so he can stay his course.

Page 62
1. P—tree branches tapped the windows, asking
2. M—She was an ice cube
3. M—The car became a bullet...it shot out
4. S—like a bull in a china shop
5. P—The table groaned
6. S—like a red cherry
7. M—The spider was a weaver
8. S—as tall as New York City skyscrapers
9. P—The waves licked
10. P—The stone skipped playfully
11. S—as busy as a bee
12. S—like a wailing siren
13. M—The moon was a spotlight
14. P—Leaves played ring-around-a-rosy
15. M—The desert is an oven

Page 70
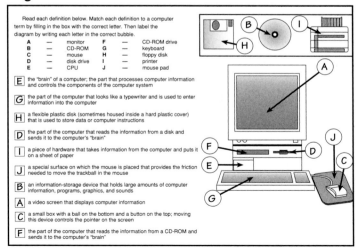

Answer Keys

Pages 80 and 81

Green (North America): Antigua & Barbuda, Bahamas, Barbados, Belize, Canada, Costa Rica, Cuba, Dominica, Dominican Republic, El Salvador, Grenada, Guatemala, Haiti, Honduras, Jamaica, Mexico, Nicaragua, Panama, Saint Kitts and Nevis, Saint Lucia, Saint Vincent and the Grenadines, Trinidad and Tobago, United States of America

Blue (South America): Argentina, Bolivia, Brazil, Chile, Colombia, Ecuador, Guyana, Paraguay, Peru, Suriname, Uruguay, Venezuela

Yellow (Africa): Algeria, Angola, Benin, Botswana, Burkina Faso, Burundi, Cameroon, Cape Verde, Central African Republic, Chad, Comoros, Congo, Coté d'Ivoire, Djibouti, Egypt**, Equatorial Guinea, Eritrea, Ethiopia, Gabon, Gambia (The), Ghana, Guinea, Guinea-Bissau, Kenya, Lesotho, Liberia, Libya, Madagascar, Malawi, Mali, Mauritania, Mauritius, Morocco, Mozambique, Namibia, Niger, Nigeria, Rwanda, São Tomé and Principe, Senegal, Seychelles, Sierra Leone, Somalia, South Africa, Sudan, Swaziland, Tanzania, Togo, Tunisia, Uganda, Zaire, Zambia, Zimbabwe

Red (Asia and Australia): Afghanistan, Armenia, Australia, Azerbaijan*, Bahrain, Bangladesh, Bhutan, Brunei, Cambodia, China, Cyprus, Egypt**, Fiji, Georgia*, India, Indonesia, Iran, Iraq, Israel, Japan, Jordan, Kazakhstan*, Korea (North), Korea (South), Kuwait, Kyrgyzstan, Laos, Lebanon, Malaysia, Maldives, Marshall Islands, Micronesia, Mongolia, Myanmar (formerly Burma), Nepal, New Zealand, Oman, Pakistan, Palau, Papua New Guinea, Philippines, Qatar, Russian Federation*, Samoa (Western), Saudi Arabia, Singapore, Solomon Islands, Sri Lanka, Syria, Tajikistan, Thailand, Turkey*, Turkmenistan, United Arab Emirates, Uzbekistan, Vanuatu, Vietnam, Yemen

Orange (Europe): Albania, Andorra, Austria, Azerbaijan*, Belarus, Belgium, Bosnia & Herzegovina, Bulgaria, Croatia, Czech Republic, Denmark, Estonia, Finland, France, Georgia*, Germany, Greece, Hungary, Iceland, Ireland, Italy, Kazakhstan*, Latvia, Liechtenstein, Lithuania, Luxembourg, Macedonia, Malta, Moldova, Monaco, Netherlands, Norway, Poland, Portugal, Romania, Russian Federation*, San Marino, Slovakia, Slovenia, Spain, Sweden, Turkey*, Ukraine, United Kingdom, Yugoslavia (Serbia-Montenegro)

* Denotes a country that is considered to be in both Europe and Asia.
** Denotes a country that is considered to be in both Asia and Africa.

Page 85

I.
Synonyms	Antonyms
pacifist	disturbance
justice	discord
respect	antagonism
cooperative	quarrel
agreement	impatience
understanding	cruelty
patience	uncooperative
tranquility	intolerance
serenity	argument
calm	chaos
truce	war
harmony	disrespect
amicable	animosity
tolerance	strife
treaty	injustice

II. Possible answers include:

respect
disrespect
dis–: not, lack of, opposite

cooperative
uncooperative
un–: not

patience
impatience
im–: lack of

tolerance
intolerance
in–: lack of

III. Answers will vary.

Page 86

Page 92

Grow It: acacia, banyan, chinquapin, citron, durra, forsythia, hyssop, liana, monkshood, whin
Feed It: addax, echidna, gaur, ibex, jerboa, kudu, oryx, urial, wapiti, zebu
Wear It: bolero, buskins, capote, cloche, fichu, gambadoes, jodhpurs, snood, ulster, wimple
Bonus Box: Possible categories include:
Bones: carpal, fibula, incus
Insects: aphid, cicada, curculio
Birds: auk, egret, heron
Minerals: azurite, mica, quartz

Page 93

1. stationary, stationery
2. lay, lie
3. consul, counsel
4. adopt, adapt
5. already, all ready
6. compliment, complement
7. confident, confidante
8. fateful, fatal
9. Set, sit
10. principal, principle
11. accept, except
12. raise, raze
13. quiet, quite
14. effect, affect
15. respectfully, respectively
16. gracious, graceful
17. capital, capitol
18. between, among
19. advice, advise
20. mania, phobia

96